Lighting the

Eye of the Dragon

Lighting the Eye of the Dragon

INNER SECRETS OF

TAOIST FENG SHUI

Dr. Baolin Wu

and Jessica Eckstein

ST. MARTIN'S PRESS ⁂ NEW YORK

For the Tao

Contents

The story of Taoist Feng Shui is a rich and ancient tapestry woven of the finest threads of Chinese culture. To study Feng Shui is to trace silken strands back through thousands of years of ceremony and tradition to a time before history, when people lived as one with nature. To hold this book in your hands is to begin a journey into realms of magic, imagination, and the vast forces of creation....

Lighting the

Eye of the Dragon

Taoist Feng Shui

Our journey begins forty years ago, one still Indian summer afternoon in Beijing. In an inner room of the White Cloud Monastery, a lively and rather bored seven-year-old boy is trying to come up with a new game to play. He's tempted, as he has been many times before, to climb up on the thousand-year-old chair said to have belonged to the legendary founder of the Dragon Gate Sect, Wang Chung Yang. Why not? The ancient chair is small. It's just about the right size for him and no one's looking. So little Wu Waize jumps up, settles himself in, and starts to rock to and fro, tilting the chair farther and farther back until—*snap*—a leg breaks and he tumbles to the ground.

Being a resourceful child, he figures he can try patching up the mess he's made before anyone discovers it. No such luck. In walks the majestic figure of his teacher, the Ancestral Grand Master of the Dragon Gate Sect, venerable Master Du.

"Up to your tricks again, boy? Instead of trying to stick that piece of wood back on with your hands, why don't you take a closer look at it?" The little boy's fright turns to amazement as he peers at the ancient calligraphy lining the hollow of the broken leg.

Traced in delicate characters, it is written, "In the fifth month of the Northern Song Shao Xing year, I, Wang Chung Yang, sit in this chair. Nine hundred and thirty seven years from today, on the fourteenth day of the eighth month, Wu Waize will break this chair in the afternoon, around five o'clock." The young boy gapes in awe. Today is September 14, 1957, and the temple bells are just striking five.

The chair now sits on display in the Museum of Chinese History, opposite the Great Hall of the People (the Chinese Parliament), in Tiananmen Square. And Wu Waize, having had his first encounter with the mystical mind of the Tao at age seven, today lives and teaches in Los Angeles, where he is a leading doctor of Chinese medicine and Qi Gong healing. Though he feels his primary responsibility to the community lies in his medical practice, Dr. Wu is a living Master of the Taoist arts and an initiate of the Orthodox School of Taoist Feng Shui (Mi Zong Feng Shui), with over forty years of study and experience. It is under his careful direction that the information in this book is being presented for the first time.

What can you call a force so far reaching that it can create a bond between a wise man from the Song Dynasty and a boy from Maoist China? What name can convey the harnessing of such power? It is *Feng Shui*.

Feng Shui is commonly understood as the practice of arranging one's living and working environments to maximize good luck, health, and success. Unfortunately, the practice is not as simple as hanging up a wind chime or moving a plant, and knowing what to put where only scratches the surface of Feng Shui—a complete worldview far different from modern ways of seeing. Originating in the shamanic traditions of ancient China and carefully preserved in secret by the Taoist masters, these secret teachings can now be revealed to the public. This book is the product of five thousand years of Chinese history.

To understand Taoist Feng Shui, the first requirement is a shift in the way one looks at the world. It must be approached with a mind-set that holds little connection to mundane, everyday thinking. Its basic concepts, though not complicated, are often difficult for the rational mind to accept. There are forces that exist in our daily lives that can be of tremendous benefit to us if we can just tune them in. Using imagination and intuition, the study of Taoist Feng Shui becomes not only a set of techniques but also an exciting exploration of our own inner potential.

Feng Shui, as commonly understood by Westerners, is the Chinese practice of positioning oneself and one's belongings within one's living and working environment in order to bring in good luck, health, and well-being. However, this technique as ordinarily taught and applied in the United States, as well as in China, tends to be filled with incomplete, incorrect, and unnecessarily intricate information. With the growing popularity of Feng Shui and the general merging of Eastern and Western cultures, Baolin Wu, Ph.D., L.A.C., renowned doctor, Feng Shui practitioner, and living master of the complete cannon of Taoist knowledge, has decided that now is the time to reveal the original teachings of Taoist Feng Shui that have been passed on to him from a 1,700-year-old oral tradition. This book will reveal an ancient system of Feng Shui that is exceptionally powerful yet profoundly simple; it stems from physical training techniques (Qi Gong) developed to produce a consciously heightened perception of oneself within the environment. The study of Taoist Feng Shui is highly recommended for anyone who seeks to unlock the mysterious connection between the body and the universe.

Before we begin our journey, let us introduce our teacher and guide, Dr. Baolin Wu. He was raised from childhood as a ward of the White Cloud Monastery in Beijing, which is considered the Ancestral Court of Taoism. As China's oldest and most central repository of the wide body of Taoist knowledge, the White Cloud Monastery is an institution comparable in scope and religious significance to the Vatican. From age four, Dr. Wu was taught and trained in Orthodox Taoism, studying in the Complete Reality and Celestial Master Schools, as well as in the Mi Zong tradition of Feng Shui. Under the direct supervision of his teacher, the Ancestral Master of the Dragon Gate Sect, Du Xinlin, Dr. Wu received a complete monastic education. He studied and excelled in Chinese medicine, Qi Gong, T'ai Chi Chuan, the martial arts, Feng Shui, and *I Ching* divination.

In the monastery, his Feng Shui studies included in-depth analyses of the major monuments of the Forbidden City, the standard features of the traditional home, as well as the layout of the city of Beijing. As a young man, he traveled extensively throughout China, Tibet, and Central Asia with his master as guide. On their pilgrimage, they traveled the route of the Great Wall, the Silk Road, finally reaching the Himalayas and the Potala Palace, stopping to analyze the many shrines and spiritual power places along the way. They observed the changing terrains, cloud formations, and wind currents, both scientifically and esoterically. Dr. Wu came away from this "Long, Long Road" with a deeply felt, firsthand encounter with Chinese history, geography, meteorology, mathematics, and astronomy—in short, with the essence of Chinese culture. Culminating the many years of theory and travel, Dr. Wu was singled out to receive the inner teachings of Feng Shui; that is, the original oral training of Qi Gong—the physical practice of opening one's body and mind to the subtle shiftings of Qi (life energy). With his forty years of continuous training and practice, Dr. Baolin Wu has become a rare figure—one who has received the complete original Taoist teachings and combined them with extensive personal experience—a true Chinese Taoist Ancestral Feng Shui Grand Master.

How can we define the function of Feng Shui? In the Chinese lan-

guage, *Feng*, literally "wind", means *Qi*, the currents of life energy that flow around and within all things. *Shui*, meaning "water," refers to money. In other words, a place's Feng Shui is a nutrient that nourishes the people who live there. People come from many different environments, which in turn create differences in appearance, personality, and culture. Feng Shui contains them all—the entire material realm. In turn, Feng Shui pervades the most minor events of our daily lives. Our careers, health, and future are affected by the environment. From the largest to the smallest facet of existence, Feng Shui is a living story, one that is constantly unfolding.

The ancient masters of Feng Shui studied the terrain and the movements of the heavens to determine the nation's fate. One of the earliest recorded texts concerning Feng Shui is Sun Tzu's *The Art of War*. Considered by the Chinese as one of the great early masters of Feng Shui, Sun Tzu's military strategies were in fact based on Feng Shui principles, and they still hold much relevance today when used for adjusting the positionings of home and office. Feng Shui lays out the campaign strategies of your own troops. When riding out to battle, you must have an understanding of the relationship of the mountains to the water and how their interaction varies as the landscape changes. If you enter a forest, you need to take precautions to prevent your enemy from cutting you off with fire. The same holds true if your house is located in an area known for brushfires. A thorough Feng Shui analysis includes a careful examination of your potential routes of escape in the case of an emergency. You can use this art of war to fight a battle or find a house. In either case, you must have an intimate understanding of your environment.

Feng Shui is far from being merely a strategic observation of the conditions of the earth; to practice Feng Shui, one must hold a mystical awareness of the workings of the universe and their manifestations here on this plane. This is the true nature of Taoist Feng Shui. Though it has its beginnings in the shamanic heritage of ancient China, Taoism as a formal movement dates back to the second century A.D., to the exalted mystic and seer, Zheng Dao Ling. As the first in a succession of Celestial Masters, he was called upon to present before the emperor the yearly forecast for the state. War, natural disasters, foreign events, and the fate of the people were all determined in rites performed at the Central Altar (Han Zhong Shi). Until the Ming Dynasty, and the arrival of the next key figure in the Taoist mysteries, Liu Bowen, the Celestial Masters continued their predictions, held apart from the influx of Buddhist thought. Their teachings, combined with those of the disciples of Liu Bowen, have been recorded in the texts of the Zheng Yi cannon. It is from these writings that the Mi Zong tradition of Feng Shui derives.

The teachings of Taoist Feng Shui have long been held secret. Very few discussions of the Mi Zong techniques exist in print. The Taoist masters felt that there were too many difficult issues involved to publish this material openly. For instance, finding disciples with the proper ethical bearing, natural ability, and discipline necessary for Feng Shui study would be no easy feat. Moreover, if the material was misunderstood or incorrectly applied, much harm could result. Another concern was the very nature of the teachings themselves. The inner awareness developed by the physical trainings could only be transmitted to the student by oral teachings given in direct demonstration and meditation by a qualified teacher. Before his passing, Dr. Wu's teacher admonished him to at last reveal this information to the public. Dr. Wu has waited nearly twenty years to bring it forth. Today's world is an open field in which the cultures of the planet meet and intermingle with a new sense of freedom and curiosity. With the teachings of Taoism being fundamentally based on freedom and inquiry, the time is right for this book.

The topics presented here are the basic principles of the practice of Taoist Feng Shui. This book is meant to be read as much from a philosophical perspective as a practical one, which is in keeping with the basic nature of Taoist thought. The methods and techniques discussed here will not turn you into an overnight master of Feng Shui. Rather, this book seeks to provide you with the resources you will need to begin your journey into this singular world as well as to help yourself, your family, and your friends. If you decide to pursue this path professionally, Dr. Wu recommends intensive study under a true teacher as the only responsible way to achieve this goal. No matter the direction of study you choose, this book will provide a fascinating window into a new way of understanding and interacting with the world around you.

Q i

From our birth to our death, we are accompanied by Qi. Qi is the living essence of the universe and the central core of the Tao. In the *I Ching*, the *Chinese Book of Changes*, the ebb and flow of Qi plays the pivotal role. The teachings of the *I Ching* reveal the interplay of the forces of nature. It is the mother of Feng Shui. To understand the meaning of Feng Shui, one must devote oneself to the study of the *I Ching* and, especially, of Qi. Feng (wind) means Qi. A leaf gently waving in the breeze is Qi. The breath in your lungs is Qi. Falling in love is Qi. If something has no Qi, then it does not exist.

How does one study Qi? Through the practice of Qi Gong, one trains one's body to become aware of its energy. Daily practice results in a heightened sensitivity to the environment and the workings of the body. With continued practice, the ability to communicate directly with the forces of nature is developed. At this point, similarities between traditional martial arts, such as T'ai Chi Chuan, and Qi Gong begin to diverge. Both can be practiced to achieve greater health and a sense of well-being. They can also result in an increased awareness of nature. Without Qi Gong, though, one is unable to enter the next stage of development, which is the return to the original, unclouded understanding of one's true nature. With this consciousness, one can take one's rightful role as a working member of the universe.

All this may sound impossible to achieve, but it's actually a very simple and natural part of human development. We all have these abilities within us. We have just lost touch with them. Qi Gong helps bring you back to yourself. This is done through sitting and standing meditations, visualizations, and breathing. There are two basic forms of Qi Gong, solar and lunar, as taught in Orthodox Taoism. The first is called the Nine Palaces, in reference to the nine openings of the body. This practice, which is done with the energy of the sun, helps increase one's bioelectric energy, and can promote a stronger immune system, as well as detoxify the body of environmental pollutants. The other principle form of Qi Gong is called the Five Centers, practiced with the moon. This practice focuses on balancing the two vertical planes of the body, regulating the internal fluids, and opening one's psychic senses. Besides these two practices, there is a wide range of other Qi Gong forms geared toward more specific results. The Qi Gong techniques presented in this book provide powerful ways of pursuing personal development with a specific emphasis on the practice of Feng Shui. They have never been introduced before to the public, and form one of the crown jewels of Qi Gong accomplishment.

Some basic information is required to understand Qi Gong procedure. First, the body has three main energy storage and transforma-

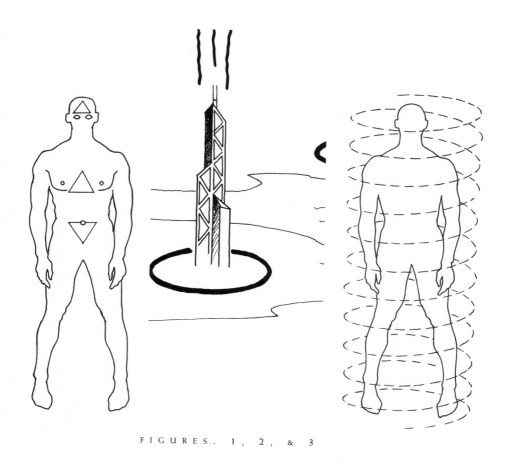

FIGURES. 1, 2, & 3

tion centers, the three inner Dan (fig. 1). The lower Dan Tian can be
located by forming your hands in the shape of a triangle with the
thumbs and forefingers touching. Place your hands over your lower
abdomen, with the tips of the thumbs at the navel. The space inside the
triangle is the exact position of your lower Dan Tian. Flip your hands
up, so the triangle is pointing up. Position it with its center at the space
between the nipples. This is the middle Dan. Strictly speaking, only
the lower Dan is referred to as the Dan Tian. (*Tian* means "field" in
Chinese, in the sense of a farmer planting seeds in a field.) Only at this
point can the process of cultivation result in the conception or creation
of new energy; hence, the usage of "Inner Field." The upper Dan is

found by placing the triangle, still pointing up, on your forehead, with the thumbs over the eyebrows and the top of the triangle touching the hairline. This position is commonly assumed to be the third eye. This is not entirely accurate. For a Taoist, the entire area above the eyebrows circling the skull is considered the body's connecting point to the messages of Heaven. Though the upper Dan plays a role in its development, the third, or Heavenly, eye uses the whole surface of the brow.

The other energy sectors to be aware of are the three central columns of energy that run vertically, the main one in the center, and the other two on each side (fig. 2). In addition, there is a field of energy that rotates around the body, encircling it from head to toe like an envelope (fig. 3). When practicing, you don't think about these centers. In fact, you don't think about anything. Instead, you let your body relax and your mind run free. This is the Taoist principle of going with the flow.

Yin and Yang

Yin and Yang are the two polarities of energy in the universe. Together, they blend to form everything in existence. Developing an understanding of the combinations of Yin and Yang and of what results from them is reached through the study of the *I Ching*. Developing a physical awareness of the substance of Yin and Yang is attained through the practice of Qi Gong. Combining this knowledge and awareness into a practical expression is the art of Taoist Feng Shui. People often ask Dr. Wu which form of Qi Gong, solar or lunar, they should do. He tells them they can accomplish anything and everything with either form. Everything has two sides, front and back, Yin and Yang.

Understanding the interplay of Yin and Yang is the crucial insight a Feng Shui practitioner must possess. Feng is wind and Shui is water. Feng represents Qi. Shui represents the flowing waters of fortune. It represents your luck and your opportunities. Feng is your Qi and water is your fortune. The two combined together as one shape your life. You must stop and remember right now, before you read any further, that Feng (Qi) is Yang and Shui (water) is Yin. The sensation of Yang is like the feeling one gets staring into a fire. Feng is Yang because it is moving constantly. Where there is movement, there is life. Light, warmth, upward motion, life—they all belong to Yang. When you are alive, you too belong to Yang. When you die, you belong to Yin. Yin is complete stillness. Lying with eyes shut, submerged in a hot bath, is not unlike the feeling of Yin. Night is Yin. Day is Yang. One constantly blends into the other. There are even Yin houses and Yang houses. Yin houses are the tombs of the ancestors, the burial grounds and the abodes of the dead. There is an entire field of Feng Shui that deals with ensuring that our departed loved ones have the best conditions for their lives in the realms beyond. This book, however, deals exclusively with the homes of the living.

In the land of the living, there is always Yin within Yang and Yang within Yin. To go a step further, in life, Yang encounters Yin even inside of the Yang of being alive. The great task of the Feng Shui master is to find the balance of Yin and Yang even as they constantly circulate and flow into each other. This is the subject of the I Ching. Every morning from 3 to 5 A.M., Dr. Wu sits and studies the I Ching. Doing so is his lifelong work. To be a master of Feng Shui, you must be able to read the I Ching like a cookbook, blending just the right proportions of Yin and Yang to achieve the desired effect. Every house, every person, every mood has its right balance. Unfortunately, the connection between the I Ching and Feng Shui is such a broad and intricate topic, we will only be able to present a tiny sampling of what it can achieve. If you find it stimulating, keep practicing Qi Gong. With patience and persistence, you will find all the answers within yourself.

Like with Like

The theory of putting like with like is one of the most ancient operations of magic, stretching back beyond the dawn of history. It is also one of the primary doctrines of Taoist Feng Shui. It operates on a principle that can be as complex or as simple as you would like to make it. Surrounding yourself with environments and objects that match your own Qi will help to bring out your fortune. It will work for you, no matter how you approach it. Throughout this book, we will explore this phenomenon through a free and intuitive approach. It can be applied in many ways to the practice of Feng Shui. Use it to look at houses, to solve problems in the Qi of an office, to read people's fortunes, and even to practice Qi Gong. It is a thread that runs the length and breath of the art of Taoist Feng Shui.

For example, in the early 1980s, the government of China debated whether to allow Britain to keep a presence in Hong Kong after its treaty had expired. The politicians wanted to ensure that if China accepted the handover in 1997, there would be a smooth transition and the fortunes of the Hong Kong economy would stay stable enough to

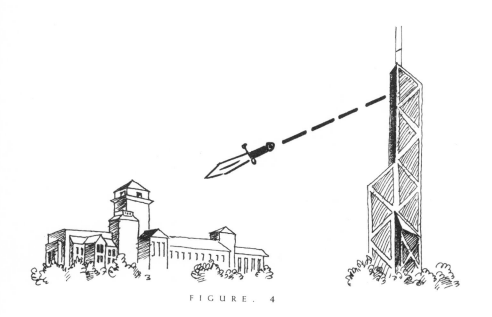

FIGURE. 4

aid the economy of China as a whole. Dr. Wu was called in as the Feng Shui consultant for the new National Bank of China, which was being designed by I. M. Pei. Dr. Wu worked directly with the architect, choosing the site and designing the appearance of the skyscraper that today graces the Hong Kong skyline with its sharply slanting roof and imposing glass edifice. Some local Feng Shui practitioners complained that the Feng Shui was all wrong. It was; all wrong for the departing government, that is. Dr. Wu designed the building like the blade of a knife and had it positioned facing the old Government Hall. This was intentionally done to cut through and overpower any factions that might remain to cause havoc (fig. 4).

A second building was built across the bay on the mainland. With this, the talisman of protection that China had long waited for was at last complete. The shape of the mountain ranges of China take the form of a dragon, its head being the island of Hong Kong (fig. 5). The two skyscrapers are positioned

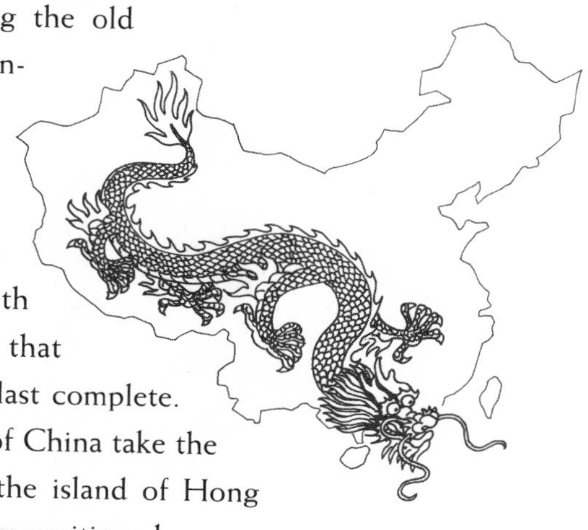

FIGURE. 5

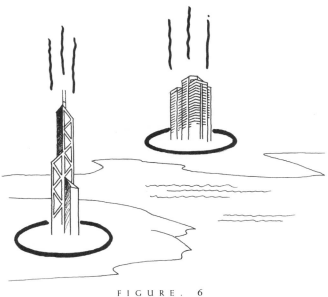

FIGURE. 6

at the exact location of the Dragon's Eyes (fig. 6). This geomantic talisman dates back to the days of the ancient Feng Shui masters, who used
huge boulders to mark the Dragon's Eyes for the safety and maintenance
of the state. Today, with its entire body at last secure and the skyscrapers in place, the Eyes of the Dragon have been lit.

Feng Shui can operate on as small or as large of a scale as is necessary. You would be surprised to know how often it is used on a grand
scale by governments all over the world. This is not something you are

FIGURE. 7

going to read about in the
morning papers. We even
have our own Dragon right
here in America. Its tail starts
at the northeastern tip of the
country and ends with its den
in California (fig. 7). Downtown
Los Angeles is its head. Dr. Wu
has taken detailed aerial photos
of the region, noting the forms

of the mountain ranges, how they go down to the sea, and the exact number of tall buildings in the downtown area. He believes that if just a few more skyscrapers can be built in L.A., the Dragon of America will open its eyes and come to life, vastly increasing the wealth and security of the nation. Don't assume this to be an exaggeration. The power of Feng Shui can take on national and even planetary dimensions.

Going with the Flow

Another aspect of keeping like with like is the idea of going with the flow. Like the passing of the seasons, every person or place has its natural rhythm that must be respected. The purpose of practicing Qi Gong and of studying the *I Ching* is to harmonize oneself with the natural world. Using your intellect and your intuition simultaneously and seamlessly, you can coordinate yourself with nature. This, for the Taoists, is the correct way to health. Going with the flow can be something as simple as wearing warmer clothes in the winter and cooler clothes in the summer. Common sense plays an important role. If you are a doctor and the seasons are changing, you know it will be time to stock up on cold remedies for your patients in advance. This way you will be able to provide them with what they need and improve your own business and earnings to boot.

The basic rule of thumb is to follow the patterns of nature. If you are careful not to go against its laws, you will reap many rewards.

Maintaining a healthy lifestyle is, of course, a part of this, but there are other, more subtle benefits. For instance, a few years ago when widespread brushfires in the hills of Malibu caused many people to lose their homes, property values in the area dropped precipitously. Yet Dr. Wu encouraged his clients to run out and purchase homes there. Some of his clients thought living in an area where fire was a common occurrence didn't seem like a wise idea. "On the contrary," Dr. Wu would tell them. "According to the principles of Feng Shui, this was an excellent plan." In the controlling cycle of the Five Elements, fire produces metal, which denotes wealth. An area with an abundance of fire has a strong potential to generate wealth for those who live there. The Five Elements—fire, metal, water, earth, and wood—are the building blocks of nature. Their actions, especially how they produce and control each other, are followed carefully by the Feng Shui practitioner. An earthquake may seem like a terrible tragedy, but the violent forces that split the earth's crust can be strong enough to bring in entirely new opportunities for the person who knows how to look for them.

The balance of Yin and Yang may at times only be changed through the intensity of confrontation. The combination of fire and water is very fortunate. They fight against each other, but when a master can bring them into balance, stasis is broken and fruitful growth may begin anew. How often do you find that after an old pattern in your life goes down in flames, the seeds of change sprout before you? If you can see these patterns in advance, you will be able to make more informed choices. If you know a coastline is unstable, buy property half a mile inland. In the future, the beach may fall into the ocean, but if it does, your property will be at the water's edge.

The distinction between incoming and outgoing energy is an important aspect of following the flow of nature. Both water and Qi course through the environment. Being able to catch the correct flow that harmonizes with your own is very important. If you make a mistake about where you stand in relation to the flow, you can seriously disrupt your life. An interesting theory recommends that if you are

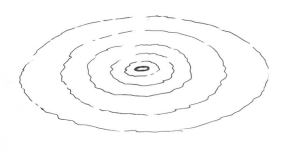

building a house, you should ask the contractor to lay the wood with its grain all running in the same direction. Scientific research in China has proven that this can balance the energy in the finished house. Flow is water. You never want to halt its motion. Remember the basic patterns of energy. All circles create further circles, like the rings that ripple outwards when a pebble is tossed in a pond (figs. 8 and 9). As in the martial arts, the vertical force breaks the horizontal force, and the horizontal breaks the vertical. One force hitting another will deflect its energy, depending on its strength and the point at which it hits (figs. 10 and 11). In this sense, two cars or two lines of Qi are the same.

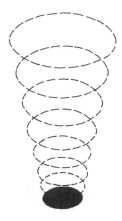

Life is a long journey. As we travel along, we may sometimes have to stop for a red light. We might have an accident. The knowledge of Feng Shui can tell us when to take a detour, or when to stop and fill up the tank. No matter what, we are still going to arrive at our original destination. To change your destiny is very difficult, but to reorder the incidentals can make the trip much more meaningful. The world of Taoist

FIGURES. 10 & 11

Feng Shui is now yours to explore. The information in this book can be used in whatever way suits you best, whether you are looking for a quick way to energize your home or searching for ultimate truths. If you come away from this material and the clouds somehow seem brighter or the song of the birds begins to whisper a poem in your ear, don't be surprised. You have begun to understand the messages of the Tao.

2

Doing the Numbers

From birth to death we are accompanied by Qi. A human life is not simply the product of sperm and egg. The Taoists believe each of us is born of both heaven and earth, conceived at the moment of perfect balance between Yin and Yang for our own individual destiny. Before creation, our original essence is formed of Ling Zi, ultra-small cosmic particles that circulate throughout the universe. At conception, our Ling is pulled down to fuse with ovum and sperm. At this instant, Ling turns to Qi. When we die, our Ling (or essence) is released to combine with all the other Ling essences in the atmosphere. Once combined, the Ling travels through the Six Realms to be born again in a new form. All balance is created from change. This is the fundamental principle of the *I Ching* and, therefore, of Feng Shui. It explains why a certain place may be good for one person but not for another. Your living and working environments must coincide with your birth time, day, and year. Ground zero is the place where you were born. It is your life's starting point.

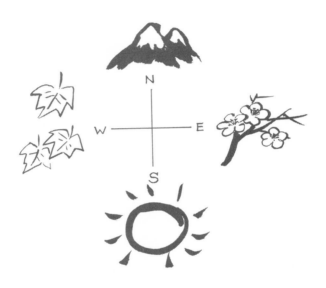

The Four Phases

In order to make harmony with heaven and earth a reality, you must begin by understanding the unique connection to time and space that exists between your birth information and the eight directions of the compass. The four cardinal directions—north, south, east, and west—are traditionally known in China as the Four Phases; they correspond to the seasons of winter, summer, spring, and fall. The season you were born in determines the direction that will bring you your greatest success, the direction in which you can best go with the flow of the Tao.

For example, let's say you were born in the spring in Los Angeles. Your birth direction would be east, the direction corresponding to spring. Los Angeles is the starting point of your life, because it is the place where you first came into the world. To find success, personal development, and advancement in life—and everything else you want to accomplish—you would go toward the east. This could mean moving to New York or just across town. In Feng Shui, this would also mean that your home and office should be oriented toward the east. The basic idea is no different than the reason behind wearing short sleeves in the summer or long sleeves in the winter. You want to move in the right direction for you, the direction that will ensure you are going with the flow. If you were born in the winter, your direction is north. If you were born in the summer, your direction is west. Remember, the place where you were born is your center. Move out from your center in your personal birth direction (fig. 12).

Your birth directions are very important when choosing a home. Generally, a good house is situated in the north with the front door facing south, or situated in the west with the front door facing east. This is an all-purpose rule of thumb. However, it is much more accurate to locate your house according to your birth direction. If you were born

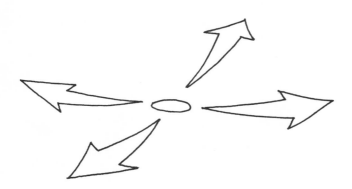

FIGURE. 1 2

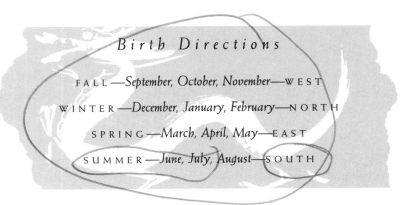

Birth Directions

F A L L —*September, October, November*—W E S T

W I N T E R —*December, January, February*—N O R T H

S P R I N G —*March, April, May*—E A S T

S U M M E R —*June, July, August*—S O U T H

in the spring, your house can be situated in the west with the front door facing east. In the same vein, if your birth season was the summer, your ideal house would be situated in the north with the front door facing south. If you were born in the spring and not only does your door face east, but your house is also situated in the east, you have formed the most fortunate position possible. This is called "double goodness." The concept of double goodness carries over to the dates of the month. The best days to move into a new place would be the first day of the first month, the second day of the second month, and so on. If instead your house is situated in the east and your front door faces south, you would have only one good, not double goodness.

Just as going with the flow helps your life, going against the flow can make things more difficult. So, still using the preceding example (birth in spring), if your house is situated in the east but your front door faces north, you have broken the flow. This combination doesn't fit together. However, if you were born in the winter, it would be good to have your front door facing north, and even better if your house was also situated in the north. This is why one house may have drastically different effects for different people.

To narrow the field even further, a very basic way to judge whether the Feng Shui of a location is particularly suited to you is to match up your address with your birth information. The numbers that make up your date of birth act as a powerful talisman. Using these numbers as a mantra for meditation can put you in touch with your original

nature. In Feng Shui, they are used according to the principle ₍
with like."

Begin with your street address. Do any of the numbers in the y
of your birth match up? If so, the more the better. If your address is 4₅
Main Street and you were born in 1963, this would be very good. For
the street address of home or office, also check the numbers of your
birth month and day. If you were born on May 3, this street address
would be excellent for you. For a large office building or apartment
complex, check your suite or apartment numbers against the numbers of
your birth month. Then, compare the numbers of rooms inside with your
birth time. If the numbers don't match, it could be a larger or smaller
problem, depending on the building's overall Feng Shui. Generally, if no
single number matches up, it may be too much of a risk to move in.
When people call Dr. Wu for a Feng Shui reading, the first thing he asks
them is if their numbers match. If none of their numbers match, he tells
them it won't be worth it to pay him to come over and take a look. This
is only a very basic technique, but it's a good place to start.

The birth seasons not only have directions attached to them; they
also have very important color correspondences. This is illustrated by

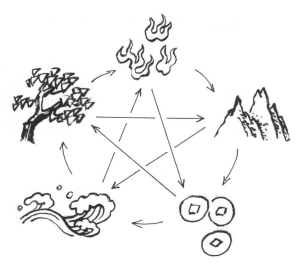

FIGURE. 13

the well-known diagram of the Five Elements (fig. 13). As discussed in the preceding chapter, understanding the interplay and exchange of the Five Elements is essential to understanding the balance of forces at work in the art of Feng Shui. If you are able to perceive their dynamics, you will gain the wisdom of nature's laws. The Taoists believe that the Feng Shui master is a doctor and that the Five Elements form the body of the master's patient, the earth.

Using your birth season's color to decorate your daily life is a simple but powerful statement of sympathetic magic. By surrounding yourself with your color, you can more fully tune into the lucky vibrations it represents for your inner self. If your birth season is fall, for instance, your birth color is white. By wearing white clothes, driving a white car, and having white furniture and carpeting in your house, you will amplify your ability to go with the flow in your own personal way. You can even bring in more fortune by choosing a pet in your birth color.

Birth Colors

Spring (February, March, April)—Wood—Green

Summer (May, June)—Fire—Red

Indian Summer (July, August)—Earth—Yellow

Fall (September, October)—Metal—White

Winter (November, December, January)—Water—Black

In general, colors can be brought into play to help achieve particular goals. The color correspondences are all derived from the *I Ching*. For example, if you are looking for a husband, wife, or lover, you want to have a lot of pink and red colors around the house. People under fifty can use lighter shades of pink. Older people looking for a mate can use darker pinks and red. A friend once asked Dr. Wu about a certain Feng Shui practitioner he had been recommended to. When the friend showed Dr. Wu the practitioner's business card, Dr. Wu told him to forget about it. The card was pink, not an appropriate color for business. It proved this person had little real understanding of the *I Ching*.

Green is a powerful color for bringing in peace and a calm life. It's also excellent for helping a career to grow. If you are not doing well financially or are out of a job, the color to spread lavishly around you is yellow. If you are sick, especially with a serious illness, avoid wearing or using black. It will make your illness worse. Use white, particularly on the walls, to help improve your condition. Wearing white clothing also aids mobility. White walls are especially good for classrooms, banks, and clinics. Using color in these ways has subtle effects, but brings noticeable long-term results. Don't disregard its power to change your life.

The Bagua

The Four Phases are the four cardinal directions—north, south, east, and west—and their correspondences in heaven and on earth. Throughout this book, we will discuss the many ways they can be used for Feng Shui. Another fundamental concept in the creation of harmony among heaven, humankind, and earth is known as the Eight Directions. On the surface these are the directions: south, southwest, southeast, north, north-west, northeast, east, and west. The Four Phases and the Eight Directions underlie the two basic truths of the universe—humanity combining with the universe as one, and the universe combining with humanity as one. These are the microcosmic and the macrocosmic ways of perceiving the world. All spiritual seekers, no matter their faith or religion, attempt to gain an understanding of these two modes of perception. For the Taoist, the study of the *I Ching* and its application in Feng Shui and Qi Gong are the roads to this consciousness.

The Eight Phases correspond to the eight basic trigrams of the *I Ching*, represented by the diagram of the Bagua. Although a full exploration of the *I Ching* is beyond the scope of our book, in this chapter we give a basic introduction to its important concepts, particularly as they relate to Feng Shui, plus a few key ideas that we will leave for the reader to ponder.

First, the evolution of the *I Ching* trigrams begins with Yin, the broken line, and Yang, the solid line. To paraphrase Lao Tze, first there was nothingness, which evolved into motion, which in turn created Yin and Yang. Yin and Yang are always moving. The object of Feng Shui is to find a balanced point within their motion, in order to create and sustain harmony. Three Yang lines are the symbol of Heaven. Three Yin lines are the symbol of earth. The Feng Shui master studies the rhythms of Heaven and earth to find this balance.

Heaven and earth are composed of various organizations of Yin and Yang that make up the remaining six trigrams (fig. 14). These are

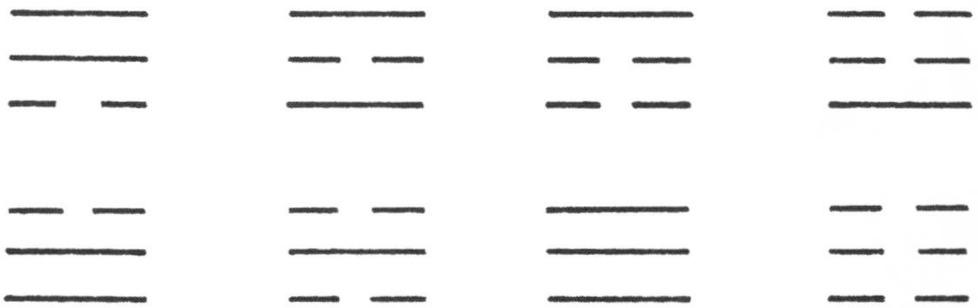

FIGURE. 14

(TOP ROW, LEFT TO RIGHT)

WIND → FIRE → MOUNTAIN → THUNDER

(BOTTOM ROW, LEFT TO RIGHT)

RIVER → WATER → HEAVEN → EARTH

Sun–Wind, Li–Fire, Gen–Mountain, Zhen–Thunder, Dui–River (commonly known in English as "lake"), and Kan–Water. As elements of the earthly plane, Qian–Heaven and Kun–Earth are also known, respectively, as Father and Mother. Each of the eight trigrams has a corresponding direction and symbolizes a wealth of areas encountered in daily living.

1. The Wind trigram (fig. 15) represents the southeast. Wind is Qi; your fortune is wafted to you on a mild breeze. Therefore, the wind trigram signifies your money and property.

FIGURE. 15

2. The Fire trigram (fig. 16) represents the south. The radiance of fire alludes to your reputation, fame, and good name. If you are looking to enhance these qualities, having a front door facing

FIGURE. 16

south is always good for your Feng Shui. Dr. Wu advised the Nixon Memorial Library to place its door in this position.

3. The Earth trigram (fig. 17) always represents the mother or the sister in *I Ching* forecasting. Its direction is southwest. If you want your mother or sister to do well, practice Qi Gong facing

FIGURE. 17

southwest. If you want to increase marital harmony or to find a suitable marriage partner, move to a house situated southwest of the starting point of your life.

4. The River trigram (fig. 18) is known as the Golden Gate. Its direction is west. It is a symbol of your children. Situating your house on a street in a location that contains two streets running straight

FIGURE. 18

with a break in the following street, just like the River trigram, will benefit your children's futures.

5. The Heaven trigram (fig. 19), symbolizing the northwest, is a sign of your father and brother. It is also the trigram of health. When consulting the *I Ching* before your father or brotherundertakes

a long trip, if this trigram appears, it will indicate the success of the journey. If it fails to turn up, travel is not recommended for them at this time. The Heaven trigram also represents very important people, usually men, who give you help and act as mentors.

6. The Water trigram (fig. 20), which symbolizes the north, concerns all issues related to your ancestor's tombs. It also is good for your career.

FIGURE. 20

7. The Mountain trigram (fig. 21) symbolizes knowledge and intellectual accomplishment. Its direction is northeast. It relates to studies and schools. It is a good sign for academic success.

FIGURE. 21

8. The Thunder trigram (fig. 22) is the symbol of the movement of Yin and Yang, and of the east. It is an important signifier of family harmony. As the trigram represents, the master bedroom

FIGURE. 22

(the Yang line) should never be squeezed between two smaller bedrooms. It should always be the last in the hall.

Numbers also play a major role in the *I Ching* and Feng Shui. Each number has a particular significance. The fortunate numbers include the following:

one—for positivity

three—for happiness and joy

five—for wealth

six—for peace and sacred emptiness

seven—for preciousness, nobility, and high rank

eight—for growth

nine—for the fusion of Yin and Yang, eternity, continuation, and luck

These numbers, which take their meanings from the *I Ching*, are used in conjunction with the trigrams to make predictions and analyze Feng Shui. Dr. Wu's explanation of an obscure Taoist text clarifies this connection. The first line, as interpreted, reads "**Heaven is one, also health; Talking is two, also explanation.**" This means the Heaven trigram represents one. It also represents health, Mother Earth, and one's homeland. This trigram is used to calculate the condition of a person's health. "Talking" refers to the River or Lake trigram.

The second line reads "**Fire is three, also radiance; Thunder is four, also movement.**" Physical fire takes the image of the Fire trigram. For Feng Shui, it is the location having two main streets and a smaller street in between, just like the shape of the trigram. Acupuncture and all health clinics, Chinese and Western, are related to fire. The Thunder trigram is movement of Yin and Yang.

The third line reads "**Wind is five, also it enters; Water is six, also it sinks.**" Wind is Qi. It should blow in like a gentle breeze. If a home or office is too windy, it can be detrimental. When it enters properly, it won't dry up the wet ground, helping wealth to accumulate. Water is wealth. As it moves inward, it fills holes in the earth, storing wealth. When looking for an office, it's often best to find one that lies below street level so that the water can flow in and fill it up. On the same theory, it is very good if your building is located next to a bank building that is higher than yours. The bank is a symbol of water and it will all flow down to you. However, if your building is taller than the bank, it won't do you any good.

The final line reads "**Mountain is seven, also it stops; Earth is eight, also it flows along with.**" Dr. Wu likens the terrain of Malibu, with its rolling hills and winding roads, to the Mountain trigram. He points out that studying the text will help one to relate one's own environment and Feng Shui needs to the trigram. The proverb ends with Earth, the exact opposite of Heaven. Again, knowing your situation will help you make the right Feng Shui choices. For example, an airline would need to keep its offices on the top floors of a tall building to be successful. A mining company, on the other hand, would need to check carefully the Feng Shui of its basement.

There are many useful applications for numbers in Feng Shui. Dr. Wu was once approached by an airline executive whose company offices were located in the same building as a competitor's offices. Dr. Wu said he didn't need to see the Feng Shui. All he wanted to know were the floors on which the two companies' offices were located. The executive's offices were located on the second floor, and the competitor's offices were on the third. This was the problem. The number 3 represents happiness and joy. The executive's company would need to move to a higher floor. The choice couldn't be an arbitrary one, though. Simply being higher up wouldn't be enough. The company would need to move to the fifth or seventh floor. The number 5 represents increasing wealth; 7 represents nobility and prestige. Together, Dr. Wu and the executive decided the company would rather target sales over fame, so the office was moved to the fifth floor.

As we have seen, the trigrams play a central role in the practice of Taoist Feng Shui. The Heaven and Earth trigrams point to the conditions of the Feng Shui, both in the sky and on the ground. The Thunder trigram helps analyze the movements of the Yin and Yang to be put in balance. The Wind trigram analyzes the Qi, and you can't have the Fire trigram working for you without also judging the condition of the Water trigram. When doing Feng Shui for the living, these are the essential trigrams.

The element of time is also critical in using the *I Ching* to analyze Feng Shui. Certain readings that would be difficult using the naked eye need to be timed for success and accuracy. For example, certain types of clouds seen in the sky can indicate mineral and oil deposits under the ground. Clouds need to be observed at a special time of the day to make a positive identification. *I Ching* calculations are made using latitude and longitude, time of the day, and observations of natural phenomena. It's not as simple as just looking up the trigrams.

Functions of Heaven and Earth

Heaven 1 gives birth to water,

Earth 2 gives birth to fire,

In Heaven 3 gives birth to wood,

On Earth 4 gives birth to metal,

In Heaven 5 gives birth to earth,

On Earth 6 results

In Heaven 7 results

On Earth 8 results

In Heaven 9 results

On Earth 10 thus becomes the center point

Another unusual Taoist text illustrates the importance of connecting the functions of heaven and earth to time of the day; as shown in the accompanying chart (see above). Here, the interplay between the cycles of the Five Elements, the hours of the day, and the resulting numerological significance is used for divination. In the passage, "Heaven . . . gives birth to water" refers to the Yin hour of 3 P.M. to 5 P.M. Six is the number for peace and emptiness of form. The meaning behind this line is that between the hours of three and five, if you have a question about the fate of an endeavor, observe certain signs related to water. If their outcome is favorable, anything you hope to achieve will be born out of the formlessness of the number 6. The interpretation of the second line is that during the hours of Yang, following the portents of fire, the spiritual nobility of heaven may rain down upon you, and so on.

After, I Ching calculations still need to be applied. This takes many years of serious study. We present this information for you to reflect upon. If you can deeply comprehend how the times and the events of daily life are the key to accurate readings of future events, you will have achieved the level of awareness necessary for the study of Taoist Feng Shui. "As above, so below" is the most basic law of nature.

3 - 6 - 7 2

By now, you may be wondering how all of this seemingly esoteric information can be put to practical Feng Shui use. The 3-6-72 formula for finding an office puts all of this information to work in a simple but very meaningful way. Created by the famous general and Taoist-adept Liu Bowen, the formula was used by him to design many of the most important structures in Beijing. The Forbidden City was built years later using Liu Bowen's plans. The Chinese name for this formula is Qian Kun Gua (the Heaven and Earth hexagram) because when properly positioned, it acts as a powerful talisman for good luck and protection. Its proportions attain the perfect balance of Yin within Yang and of Yang within Yin.

To begin with, 3-6-72 stands for 3 streets, 6 alleys, and 72 buildings. The formula contains all the numbers of good luck. The number 3 is for happiness, and 6 is for peace. The number 72 is broken down into 8 x 9 = 72, and then 8 + 9 = 17. The number 1 is Heaven, 7 is nobility, 8 is growth, and 9 is eternal continuation. The numbers 1, 3, 6, 7, 8, and 9 are the positive, growth-oriented numbers, all contained in one formula. The object is to position your chosen office at the center of three vertical streets and six horizontal streets, with thirty-six carefully observed buildings on either side.

The first step involved is determining the trigram that relates to your business, and then breaking down the map of the area you are trying to find a space in into trigrams as well. The details of this initial operation are beyond the scope of this book, but it only adds another level of accuracy to a formula that is already highly effective. To describe this operation very briefly, let's assume you want to open an acupuncture clinic in Santa Monica. Acupuncture needles are related to metal and the number 10. The element of Fire controls metal, so you would need to find an area on the map that corresponds to the Fire trigram in order to start your search. In Santa Monica, you would note that the downtown area has twenty-three streets running in a north–south direction. The streets are divided into groups of three, each assigned its own trigram. First Street to Third Street would be one trigram, Fourth Street to Sixth Street would be another trigram, and so on. Every six streets contain one pre-Heaven trigram and one post-Heaven trigram (fig. 23). You would start mapping the street from the ocean, which is Yin and which corresponds to the Water trigram. First Street would therefore be a broken line, and Second and Third Streets would be solid lines. The following three streets would be matched to the following trigram around the wheel, but from the post-Heaven configuration. This would be the Fire trigram. Fourth and Sixth Streets would be Yang lines, and Third Street would be Yin. The trigrams

FIGURE. 23
(LEFT WHEEL) PRE-HEAVEN CYCLE
(RIGHT WHEEL) POST-HEAVEN CYCLE

would continue to be laid down, one pre-Heaven, one post-Heaven, until all twenty-three streets were mapped. The cross streets would also have to be properly mapped. After looking at the total picture, you see that Second, Third, Fourth, Sixth, Ninth, and Fourteenth Streets would be the best locations for the acupuncture clinic. Remember, this is only a rudimentary description of a complex process. It takes great skill and experience to set up this map properly.

Whether or not you have pinpointed the perfect street based on the trigram map, now is the time to look at the building where you want your office to be located. The street your building is on is the first of the three streets. The other two are the streets that run parallel to yours, one on each side. These are the three "horizontal streets" (fig. 24). The six "vertical" alleys are the three streets that run perpendicular on each side of the block where your building is located. (fig. 25). If you notice, you have now formed the Earth trigram and the Heaven hexagram. You have created a powerful grid of Yin and Yang energy that surrounds your office (fig. 26).

The final test is in the thirty-six businesses or houses on either side of your office (fig. 27). You need to take a walk down your street, crossing intersections if necessary. Look at the condition of the thirty-six buildings that flank yours on each side. Are they all prosperous and lively looking, or are a few closed down or vacant? If all seventy-two

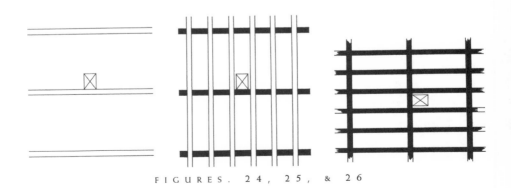

FIGURES. 2 4 , 2 5 , & 2 6

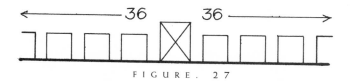

stores or houses are thriving, then you have just found your new office. If some of them look empty or run down, you will need to find another location, maybe one further up the street or on a different street entirely. It's very important to follow this formula strictly. If you combine this placement with a check to see that the numbers of your address properly match your birth date information, and that the front door faces in the correct direction, you will have created your talisman. The chances are very low that you won't succeed in your business.

When Dr. Wu was in Las Vegas, consulting on the design and placement of a major casino on the Strip, he used this formula. The only problem was that because of the way Casino Row is situated, he could only count streets and alleys to the left. To the right was open desert. Dr. Wu improvised and counted electric poles instead, but he warned the casino owners to continue their business at this location for seventeen years only. After that, they would never turn a profit again unless they moved on. Dr. Wu has used this method to situate important projects both here and abroad, including the new international airport being planned in Beijing. The Bank of China Building (the Eye of the Dragon mentioned in the previous chapter) was positioned entirely on this principle as well.

Whenever you look for an office, you should follow this formula. This is the technique that most exactly combines the *I Ching* with Feng Shui. The 3-6-72 practice alone encompasses the entire range of Chinese divination, numerology, Feng Shui, and Taoist philosophy. Dr. Wu's master had wanted to write a book entitled 3-6-72 that would only explore this one method. This talisman forms the connection between Heaven and Earth, with your office firmly planted at its center. Once you have found your correct spot on the grid, you have become the Eye of the Dragon.

Testing the Wind

Once you have positioned an office, the next thing you will need to do is test its Qi. Qi is wind and money is water. Excess wind will dry up your environment and rob you of the moisture you need to accomplish your goals. Even without a thorough knowledge of the *I Ching*, there are many sensing practices that can be easily learned. Some of them, discussed in Chapters 4 and 5, are Qi Gong forms that require perseverance and steady practice. To test the Qi is a much simpler operation. Both of these techniques can be done for your friends and family.

The first way of testing the wind for someone is to stand together inside of the office, looking out the open front door onto the street, hallway, or courtyard. Next, suggest that the two of you step outside for a minute. You take three steps out of the office door. This corresponds to the 3 of 3-6-72. Then, turn to face south. This represents 6. Relax all the joints and muscles in your body. This is 72. In this position you check to see if it's windy or not. The most important thing to remember is to check for the wind only during the two-hour period that corresponds to your friend's birth animal. You need to casually ask your friend about his or her birthday and age. Then you can look up the animal hours at home and know when to come.

If your friend's animal hours land in the middle of the night, you can come during the corresponding hours in the daytime. If your friend is a Tiger, for example, you are probably not going to be testing the wind at four in the morning. Come over between three and five in the afternoon instead. If it's mild with a gentle breeze when you test the wind, it's good. If it's very windy, it's not good. But remember, the only wind that is important is the wind blowing during your friend's animal hours.

Animal Hours

11PM-1AM	— Rat		11AM-1PM	— Horse
1AM-3AM	— Ox		1PM-3PM	— Sheep
3AM-5AM	— Tiger		3PM-5PM	— Monkey
5AM-7AM	— Rabbit		5PM-7PM	— Rooster
7AM-9AM	— Dragon		7PM-9PM	— Dog
9AM-11AM	— Snake		9PM-11PM	— Pig

Another common technique that Dr. Wu learned from his teacher is the best one to use if your friend's office opens onto a windowless hallway, where air isn't coming in from the outside. Meet your friend at the office during the proper time. Ask your friend to step outside the office with you. Take three steps outside and then do anything you can to get your friend to face south while touching the wall. If the wall is narrow and you can only take two and a half steps, that's okay. If you can't take even those few steps, you are already having a bit of a Feng Shui problem. In any case, your friend is facing south leaning on the wall. You are facing north looking at him. A good way to lure your friend into this position is for you to lean up against the wall yourself. Friends will often mirror each other's body language without even thinking about it.

Once your friend is facing south and is touching the wall, relax your muscles and joints as before, and have a little chat. Observe the hem of his shirt to see whether it moves or not. It doesn't matter exactly what position you're standing in or what you talk about. Just look for the movement (fig. 28). Sometimes a Taoist will have the person move around, do Qi Gong, or do some other motion. But the practitioner is really just observing the hem of the shirt. With this process, you are seeing the Qi. If there's no movement at all, this place is not good. If

there's some motion, it's good. This is called Human Harmonized with Heaven.

As we stress throughout this book, checking Feng Shui is not as simple as taking a look at how healthy the plants are. If there's a dead animal in the ground, the plants are going to be nicely fertilized but that won't have anything to do with the Qi. If you want the plants to look fuller, just give them some fertilizer and they will grow. You can't control the way the bottom of your shirt moves, though, especially when you don't know it's being watched. Some of the methods discussed in this book are commonly known to people interested in Feng Shui. But these techniques for reading the wind are Taoist secrets that have never before been taught publicly. They reveal the secrets from heaven. This is why when you do this reading for your friends, they can't be told in advance.

FIGURE. 28

A similar situation is found when trying to determine whether a pregnant woman is carrying a boy or a girl. Dr. Wu watches her as she is walking out the door and then abruptly calls her name so she looks back over her shoulder. If she looks to the left, the baby is a boy. If she turns to the right, it's a girl. You can't tell her this mystery ahead of time. It is the spontaneous moment that most perfectly reveals the Qi. This is fundamental to the Taoist perspective.

To clarify a few points, if your friend has his shirt tucked in, look at the cuff of his sleeve. If his shirt is sleeveless, look at the bottom of his shorts or pants. For a woman, look at the hem of her skirt. Also, if the door already faces south, turn to the east. South and east are Yang directions. Never face north or west. These directions are the Yin, which is still, with no movement. For an apartment, office, or house, do the wind test at the front door, not at the front gate or in the lobby.

The front door carries 80 percent of the weight in a Feng Shui reading, compared to 20 percent for a gate or lobby. This is because you are right inside of your front door, living and working. It is the entrance to your opportunities.

This chapter has illustrated some of the complexities of Taoist Feng Shui. The *I Ching* can be very complex in its mathematical expression of the wisdom of the earth. However, just remember that the *I Ching* speaks from the ground. With sensitivity, you can learn to hear its messages, even without the calculations. The true purpose of this book is to bring you into the spontaneous world of Feng Shui.

3

Sensing the Qi

Have you ever visited a certain person or place with a young child only to watch helplessly as your little one melts into tears or explodes with an anxious burst of hyperactivity? Remember that creepy old house that none of the neighborhood kids would go near? Dr. Wu can't count the number of times he has consulted with families who say, "Ever since we moved into the new house, our child hasn't stopped crying." Everyone has childhood experiences of spooky sensations, invisible friends, or "bad men" coming to get them. If you think back hard enough or ask people who knew you when you were small, chances are you would come up with quite a list of such memories.

There is a very good reason for all this. The *I Ching* emphasizes that the two main indicators of cosmic conditions are young children and birds. Both children and birds play a central role in forecasting and divination, fortune-telling, and Feng Shui analysis. Their close connection to the universal flow allows them to act as conduits for divine information; birds by their flight through the sky, children by their intrinsic spirit and energy. In the Tao, the ways of a child reveal the messages of heaven.

In 1966, shortly before the beginning of the Cultural Revolution, Dr. Wu's teacher, Master Du, took him aside to tell him that China was soon going to be in the throes of revolution. Dr. Wu asked his teacher how he could know such a thing. His response was, "It's part of the *I Ching*. You can predict things." Master Du then asked his student what he had seen that morning on the way to school. The young Dr. Wu said there had been a group of children playing with a top, a common toy on the streets of Beijing, whipping it with a string to keep it spinning. Master Du explained that the way they whipped the top was like the whipping of people, the capturing of people; this was the sign. It is the will of heaven to warn us ahead of time about everything that will happen, whether we realize it or not. The study of Feng Shui and of the *I Ching* is an attempt to recognize these messages ahead of time.

At times, these advance warnings are displayed clearly by the forces of nature. For example, before it rains, it will first be windy and dragonflies will fly low in the sky. Ants will break their formation and rush about looking for cover. Before an earthquake, dogs, cats, and rats will jump about and behave aggressively. These are warnings that heaven gives to us. In other instances, the message may come in a less obvious or logical way. As in the preceding account of children whipping a top, the direction of a country's economy can be foreseen from the most popular games and toys that its children are enjoying. This is a Taoist perspective. With all his years of experience, Dr. Wu is convinced of the accuracy of this connection. It just takes a different way of looking at things.

Right now, you see a lot of kids with skateboards. Dr. Wu feels this hasn't been such a good sign. Having a lot of skateboarders could point to the possibility of an unstable economy. Skateboarding is an unsteady sport, involving lots of jumps and bumps. The more skateboarding you see going on, the greater the chance of the U.S. economy going down. As a matter of fact, as the skateboard craze has died down somewhat in the past couple of years, the economy has stabilized. Is there a way to explain this phenomenon logically?

A few years ago, as a student of Dr. Wu, I often practiced Qi Gong at a local park a block away from a grammar school. I'll never forget how often I overheard the second and third graders who stood nearby watching me. One would invariably stage-whisper, "What's she doing?" while the other would reply, "Shh! She's meditating." I was struck by how such young children could instinctively recognize what I was doing. While nonplussed adults would come up to me asking if I had lost something, these eight-year-olds would stand by in curious but respectful silence. Then it occurred to me, these kids were thoroughly steeped in Teenage Mutant Ninja Turtles comics, and martial arts video games. By osmosis, they were absorbing an awareness of Eastern culture. Maybe there was something good about those Saturday morning *Kung Fu* cartoons after all. Respecting children as representatives of our collective unconscious is a valuable lesson to learn.

Of course, the Taoists have been aware of this lesson for hundreds of years. But having a psychological insight into it is only the first step. Finding a practical way to apply it to benefit your life involves taking the insight to another level. Whatever a child plays at or with will be what the nation builds or develops. How do you put this concept to use?

While Dr. Wu was visiting a friend at his home, the friend asked if he should buy some stock he had his eyes on. Right at that moment, Dr. Wu observed this man's son out in the backyard playing with a hula hoop. Being in the moment and accepting the signs of heaven as they come, Dr. Wu advised his friend not to invest his money in the stock. The hula hoop spinning around and around, throwing energy outward off of it but going nowhere in a closed circle, was the symbol of the failure his friend would have if he played the market at that time. If the boy had been playing with blocks or building and constructing something, it would have indicated his father's success in the venture.

Some time later, the friend called Dr. Wu to ask again if now was the right time to buy. Dr. Wu asked him what time it was. It was four o'clock in the afternoon. Then he asked what the friend's son was doing at that moment. He was taking a nap. Dr. Wu asked if the boy had wet the bed in his sleep. The answer was no. Dr. Wu told his friend to go ahead and buy as much stock as he wanted.

How did Dr. Wu know? The *I Ching* correspondences were his guide. Using the paradigm of the functions of Heaven and Earth shown in Chapter 2 (page 31), he checked the time and the position of the boy in the house. From this he could analyze what action would be best to take. In this case, as the chart says, "Heaven 1 gives birth to water," from three o'clock to five o'clock is the Yin hour, giving birth to water. Four o'clock being in this time frame, this is when he would ask if the

Exercise

1. Turn back to the charts in Chapter 2 and read through each one again.
2. On a piece of paper make a list of all the things a young boy would do in a day—his toys, his games—and whether he would be happy, sad, sleeping, or running around.
3. See if you can find a corresponding line in the *I Ching* chart "Functions of Heaven and Earth" for each one of your little boy's actions.

child had wet the bed. No wet nappies meant water (Yin) was conserved, so he could move on to the next part of the line—"On Earth 6 results." It is at this time of absolute emptiness that you can plant the seed of your wishes. Whatever you think can become a reality. This is the true method of the I Ching in action. The forecasting is all based on calculations, but the most important information—the source material—comes from observing everyday life.

Children and Feng Shui

Observing children in order to make divinatory predictions is not an easy technique to explain. Making accurate I Ching calculations based on the observation of natural phenomena, such as the behavior of children, requires many years of study and experience. Also, the more one studies, the more complex the studies become. We have presented this basic information primarily as a way to jump into the spontaneous, intuitive mind-set so fundamental to Taoist Feng Shui. However, letting children help you to check a home or office is, hands down, the easiest method of Feng Shui. To determine if a site is good or not good, just bring a little boy along with you when you go there to look.

Put him in the garden or yard, if there is one, or put him in a room and close the door. Give him some toys to play with and wait about twenty minutes. Then observe his behavior or ask him whether he wants to play some more. If he is happy and willing to stay longer, playing away contentedly, then you know this is a good spot. If he cries or says he is scared, or if he obviously doesn't want to be there, then you don't want to be there either. If he asks for a drink of water or wants to go to the bathroom, that is a bad sign as well. The place is not good.

Children feel and see many things that adults cannot. If there's a problem with the Qi in a house, the first people to be affected by it will usually be the young children. A few years ago, Dr. Wu received an unusual case at his clinic involving a baby with a strange condition.

The child's parents were research scientists, the father at Cal Tech and the mother at MIT. Every night, the little boy would run a fever so high he often went into seizures, but by the time his parents would rush him to the hospital, the baby would be fine. The usual battery of tests would be run and the results would all come back normal. Once the boy would be brought home, the fever and all the symptoms would return in full force. So back and forth to the emergency room he would go. The doctors then recommended an overnight stay. In the hospital that night, for the first time, the baby slept soundly.

Finally, one day, the boy had a particularly bad attack. His grandfather, who stayed with the boy during the day, called the boy's father in a panic, begging him to come home quickly. The father was in the middle of an experiment and couldn't leave the laboratory, so he told the grandfather to take the baby to Dr. Wu as a last-ditch effort. Dr. Wu checked the child's pulses and everything was normal. It was time to put his Taoist training to work. He wove sewing needles into the corners of the baby's shirt and sent him home. Some time later, the boy's father came to the clinic to tell Dr. Wu that from that day on, the baby's symptoms had disappeared and had not returned. Because of his scientific interest, he questioned Dr. Wu about the unusual nature of the care. All Dr. Wu could tell him was that some things can't be helped by a medical solution.

According to Taoist belief, the baby's house was unclean. A baby's energy is pure Yang. If Yin Qi is present in a sufficient quantity, it can invade the child's Yang Qi, creating an abnormal response. *Yin Qi* refers to a whole range of energetic entities that emanate from astral planes and the realm of the dead. These forces are not necessarily evil, but they do not belong in the land of the living and can block the flow of healthy Yang energy. A major role of a Taoist Feng Shui master is to purify unclean Qi, thereby preventing the realms of the living and the dead from overlapping. We will explore this topic in depth in Chapter 4.

Although children, being so thoroughly Yang, are most likely to attract Yin Qi, adults can be affected by it as well. If you feel there might be something wrong, place sewing needles on the hems of children's shirts. For adult men, stick a needle through the left-hand collar of the shirt. For adult women, pin the collar on the right-hand side. The sharp needles act as talismans to repel unclean forces. Dr. Wu has used this technique many times and finds it works very well.

The more Yang a child is, the more sensitive he will be to Yin energy. This is why, as a firm rule, the child you use for forecasting or observing Feng Shui must be a young boy. A little boy is pure Yang; no Yin at all. He should be under the age of seven, but in a pinch, he can be nine or younger. Your reading will be less accurate if he's older than seven, and if he's older than nine, it won't work at all. A young girl, having a mixture of Yin and Yang from the earliest age, will also not be the best source for an accurate reading. Being partially Yin, Yin Qi will be less likely to make a subliminal impression upon her. This is a law of the I Ching.

To be sure, the I Ching recognizes the role of feminine energy. The Yin energy that comes forth from women makes them ideally suited to be teachers and psychologists; more suited, in fact, than men. This is also based on calculations from the I Ching. Mental problems and aggressive behavior stem from imbalances in the heart center (xin zhong). The heart relates to fire, and the aggressive urges are expressions of fire. Water needs to be used to control fire, and water is the female principle. Therefore, female therapists and healers are preferable to extinguish mental illness, and to impart teachings in an emotionally connected, holistic way.

Generally speaking, every individual and situation must contain a harmonious balance of Yin and Yang energy. To sense Feng Shui accurately, though, requires undiluted Yang energy and an ability to bring out the messages from heaven. Bringing a little boy under the age of seven along to feel the Qi of a prospective house or office will be more accurate than having a Feng Shui practitioner come over to look. In essence, a true master of Feng Shui must possess, above all, the sensitivity and life force of a child.

Heaven and Human United

Taoist thought has contemplated the connections among humanity, nature, and heaven for thousands of years. Exploring the interrelation of the macrocosm and the microcosm is the ultimate purpose of Taoist Feng Shui. On the most absolute level, the universal and the human planes combine as one. This is the outside view looking inward, the cosmic perspective coming from the universe's point of view. On this level, we can never predict what will happen. In the sky, sunshine can change to clouds and rain. The four seasons shift in an endless procession. Can we ever really know why? Humans cannot calculate the decrees of heaven.

The ancient general and Feng Shui master, Zhu Ge Liang, in a fateful battle recounted in *The Romance of the Three Kingdoms*, drew up a mighty battle map. He called on the forces of wind and mountain and fire. He created a plan from which the enemy could be trapped in a mountain valley, and then destroyed by fire. The day of the attack began. Everything was going according to the general's calculations, but then it rained. A torrential downpour doused the bonfires, and the enemy's general and his son were able to escape. His soldiers wanted to give chase, but Zhu Ge Liang called them off. He told them, "The heavens don't want them to die." Destiny is created by heaven. A wise

Feng Shui practitioner understands and accepts that as much he or she can improve a situation, some mysteries must be left unknown.

An area that can be more easily studied is the realm of heaven and earth combined. This is the world of natural phenomena that paints our environment with its unique colors. Different environments produce different flowers, different animals, and different people with different colors of hair and skin and in different sizes. In China, the women of one province are known for their singing and in another they are known for their dancing. Different areas bring out different talents in their inhabitants.

The sun shines down upon the north and the south differently. This is why their crops are different. In the south there are two rice harvests, and in the north there is one. Although the north has only one rice crop, it has the finest soybean crop in the world. Idaho is famous for its potatoes and France for its wine grapes. Each country and each place has its own specialties. When you look at Feng Shui, you must take these things into consideration.

Different cultures, different areas, and different places all combine to create different people. Dr. Wu prescribes different medicines to people of different backgrounds. A Chinese patient and an American patient with the same illness are not the same. The American patient's digestive tract may be longer and the Chinese patient's shorter. The prescription therefore must be adjusted. Dr. Wu treats not only humans but also animals—from pet dogs to tigers in the zoo. Because he takes the size difference into consideration, he is able to treat them all safely and effectively.

This way of seeing also applies to Feng Shui. Noticing differences and similarities with a discriminating and imaginative eye should become a daily habit for the student of Feng Shui. This is the principle of Tong Qi—like seeks like—in action.

Take, for example, the art of reading a person's fortune by looking at the person's appearance. There are five special "looks." If the person looks like an animal or a plant, this will indicate an unusual personality or characteristic. For example, similar to the plant or animal he or she resembles, a person who looks like a cat is sneaky or tricky, while a person with long arms and big ears like a monkey will be very noble. (The ancient emperors were always said to have these features.) A woman with a wiggle in her walk like a snake will have lots of money. The other four of the five looks involve opposites interacting with each other. If a man looks like a woman, he will have great good luck. If a woman looks like a man, she will have good luck later in life, after the age of fifty. If a child looks like an old person in miniature, a long life will be had. Finally, if an old person looks very young, this is a sign of long life and good luck. All this may be very amusing, but using a person's "look" can be quite accurate. It's also a good way to loosen up and fine-tune your powers of observation.

The Five Forests

The Five Forests are the five essential signs of "Heaven and Earth United." Feng Shui is the art of environment and the Feng Shui master is its doctor. Traditionally, a doctor that strives to heal his or her patients is, in Chinese wordplay, likened to a tree. Modern science has proven the way in which the forests of the earth release life-giving oxygen. Similarly, the elements of the Five Forests emit Qi into the world. They are the primary indicators of Feng Shui.

The Elements of the Five Forests

The forest of the heavens is the clouds.

The forest of the earth, the soil.

The forest of the mountains is the rocks.

The forest of the rivers, water.

The forest of the trees is the birds.

THE FOREST OF THE HEAVENS

The number-one requirement for being a Feng Shui master can be simply put: You must be able to read Qi. Dr. Wu has some friends he does Feng Shui with, and when they get together, they take walks around the neighborhood and talk. Sometimes his friends will point to a house and say, "Hey, the Feng Shui looks good over there. The trees and plants all look so healthy." Usually, Dr. Wu has to tell them, "You're wrong. There's a dead animal buried under there. Of course the plants look good—they're being fertilized. If you go to the cemetery, everything looks nice and green too, but it's not a good place to live." Landscaping is not an accurate measure of Qi. To read Qi, you must first look up to the sky.

Remember, Feng = wind = Qi. Start feeling the Qi. It must feel mellow and warm and soft, with a gentle breeze blowing. Then check for clouds. If a place has no clouds, it's not good. When looking at a house, store, or office, there must be clouds floating in the sky above it. Dr. Wu was once asked to do a Feng Shui reading for a piece of property where a family was planning to build a house. When the family members arrived, the doctor didn't even get out of the car. He advised them not to use this place. They asked why and he told them that not only were there no white clouds, but also the Qi itself was black. He said there was no way they could live there. The clients thought that was a silly answer and went ahead and built their house there anyway. Shortly after the house was built, a serious misfortune befell their daughter. After the tragedy, they ended up selling their million-dollar house at a substantial loss. However, having a cloud of black Qi hovering about is beneficial for casinos, racetracks, and shady businesses that make easy money by luring people to squander their cash. There are always two sides to the same coin.

"As above, so below" is an idea that is well illustrated by the observation of clouds. The colors and forms of clouds can mirror conditions below the surface of the earth. In 1971, when Dr. Wu was still a young medical intern, he was asked by some friends to help in a government effort to locate new oil deposits in Tianjing. The area being surveyed was extensive, and there had been problems deciding where to begin test drilling. They were taking Dr. Wu for a drive through the fields when suddenly he told them to stop. He got out of the car, pointed to a spot, and told them they would find their oil field right there. The location was staked off, and the drilling hadn't gone very far before they struck oil. There was general amazement and though they knew it had to do with his training from the White Cloud Monastery, they still asked him how he had known where to look. Dr. Wu told them, "It's easy, just look up. The sky is blue but the clouds above this spot are black. So, of course, there's oil here. It's that simple."

Black clouds that don't disperse in a clear sky are the sign of oil underground. Dr. Wu has also located gold in America for a private mining concern. All he did was look for a location with a reddish tint in the light and some yellow clouds. What's the connection? It's so simple it's easily overlooked. The Five Elements are reflected in the sky. When you see the outside, you see the inside. If you want to know what's underground, look up in the sky to find out. This is a special untold Taoist secret from the White Cloud Monastery, and one that even a young child can grasp.

There are many different types of clouds. According to the *I Ching*, different clouds appear at different times. The best thing to do if you find a place you like, is to go back and observe the clouds a few times on different days and at different times of the day. If you hire a Feng Shui practitioner and he or she stops in only once for a little while, the reading won't be very accurate. It would be much better if the practitoner could return periodically over the course of a few days or weeks. In some circumstances, Dr. Wu might only check a location's Feng Shui once; but in these cases, he makes calculations from the *I Ching* based on the birth information, picking a special time to come and gather information about the clouds. At that precise moment, he can collect all the clouds' information and put it in a hollow Taoist gourd. Yet again, the practice of Feng Shui is not always so easy to relate to. You have to practice Qi Gong, read the *I Ching*, and calculate the mathematics involved. Nevertheless, as intricate as deep study of Feng Shui can be, you can just as well take its mysteries on a simple level and still be accurate.

THE FOREST OF THE EARTH

Earth's forest is the soil beneath our feet. Tiny seeds put into the ground and moistened with just the right amount of water will grow into tall, healthy plants. This is the life-giving power of Yin. However, subterranean currents of decomposition and death also come from underground. You need to check the Qi of the earth around your house to see if it's healthy or unclean. Qi Gong practice makes your entire body sensitive to the energy coming up from under the ground, but grabbing a handful of dirt and giving it a squeeze will also give you plenty of information to go by. Check a handful of dirt from each corner of your house. Does it look rich and black? Feel its consistency. If it's too wet or too dry, it's not good for you. You want to feel a sort of springy quality in the soil. Squeeze it a little in your palm and then open your hand. It shouldn't crumble apart loosely, but it also shouldn't clump together in a thick, sticky mass either. It should spread out, but not fall apart—like a good pastry dough. You can even taste the soil on the tip of your tongue. If it has a sour flavor, there's something wrong. Don't overlook the humble mud in your hands.

If you ask a Feng Shui master to look at your house and you notice that after he has walked around it several times, his hands are still clean, don't pay him. You can taste the difference between a flaky, hand-rolled pie crust and machine-made dough. It's all in the hands. You have to use them to look at the mud. If you never bend down to feel the dirt, you will regret it for the rest of your life.

THE FOREST OF THE MOUNTAINS

The forest of the mountains is made of rock. What type of rock? Rock that is alive. It's easy to see the difference between a live tree and a dead tree, but it takes practice to do the same with a rock. Qi Gong training develops your ability to perceive the life force that flows through everything in the natural world. I believe that anyone can, over time, get to this level. Once you have learned the proper techniques, all it takes is patience, a good heart and practice, practice, practice. Until then, a good starting point with rocks is to pick them up, just like the dirt, and observe what you feel. A living rock will have a certain brightness around it that a dead rock won't. When you look at it, you should see movement and force coming up from within. Also, the rock should be delicately shaped and good-looking.

"People with wisdom favor the water. People with ethics favor the mountains. When you pile up the earth, you form a mountain. Before it rains, smoke and fog collect on the mountain tops." This is a teaching from the *I Ching*. From a Feng Shui perspective, this passage refers to a living rock's ability to collect Qi. Having a few live rocks around your house brings in energy and "ethical" vibrations. Having wall-to-wall carpeting all through the house is not that good. Stone and marble flooring will accumulate more Qi. If you practice Qi Gong or the martial arts, you have to be around rocks. Don't ever practice Qi Gong inside the house on carpet. Dr. Wu's teacher even went so far as to tell him never to wear socks. Practice Qi Gong outside on bare ground or inside on a stone or wood floor, but never on carpet. This will help you to fully absorb the earth's energy.

THE FOREST OF THE RIVERS

Streams, rivers, oceans—their forest is the water. Water is your fortune. Water should be sparkling and clear, moving and circulating, splashing and bubbling. Avoid dark, stagnant water no matter where you are. Dams and canals block water's natural flow. They are not good. Even a fish tank in your house should have a pump to keep the water circulating.

When Dr. Wu did the Feng Shui for a major casino in Las Vegas, he used the principle of flowing water. Water represents fortune and children represent water. The more children around, the more fortune there will be. Dr. Wu recommended that the first floor be designed with plenty of colors and lights that would appeal to kids aged nine years and under. Young children under nine are water. The second floor was designed for the fourteen and under set, to continue the flow upward. The video arcade was placed there, to attract the older children's energy.

THE FOREST OF THE TREES

Of everything I have learned from Dr. Wu about Feng Shui, my favorite image is of a vast tree blanketed in a forest of brightly colored songbirds. It always puts me in a peaceful, happy mood. The Taoists believe that birds are the messengers of heaven. Soaring through the sky on light currents of air, warbling clear, ringing notes with their tiny throats, birds obviously have a unique connection to Qi. They have specially developed abilities to sense the Original Qi of the universe. The majority of *I Ching* calculations are based on the flight paths of birds. To choose the proper timing of an event in advance, you must observe the behavior of the birds and the direction they fly in at the same time as your intended action. Based on this information, you can determine through further calculation whether the timing is right and whether there will be a positive outcome. Conversely, if you have an unusual encounter with a bird, you can check the exact time and use that data to make predictions as well. These are some of the most secret marvels of *I Ching*.

Birds' heightened responsiveness to Qi makes them your helpers in Feng Shui. If you have a lot of trees on your land and never see a wing or hear a chirp, there is something very wrong. When we are born, we are connected to our true natural energy, our "Original Qi." The pressure of living in a world filled with power struggles builds up Ba Qi (stopped Qi). Wild birds are particularly sensitive to Ba Qi, and this is why they usually fly off before humans get too close. A three-foot distance is common. If there are rarely any birds around at all, though, it's time to check for problems. Conversely, if there are plenty of birds, you look to see what types they are. The more beautiful and better singing varieties are the best types. Check for birds at dawn. If a lot of birds are out singing vigorously at dawn, it's a good sign.

The Five Forests are the basic building blocks of the environment. They reveal to us heaven's manifestation in nature, if only we are able to see it. We are now ready to discover that way of seeing.

4

Human and Universe Unite

The central principle of Taoist Feng Shui is the establishment of the connection among Heaven, Human, and Earth. This is accomplished by the practice of Qi Gong. Working with the Qi, a student of Feng Shui learns to unite body and mind with the shifting combinations of heaven and earth. These training practices are very simple but have profound and immediate effects. Performed with concentration and conviction, they discipline the mind, develop ethical qualities, and harmonize the body with nature at a deep level. With daily practice, you can achieve noticeable levels of sensitivity to the environment and intuitive insight into its workings. Continued over a longer period, you can increase your health and vitality, strengthen your astral and spiritual bodies, and come in contact with heavenly forces beyond the mortal plane. Your energy becomes a blessing to all it touches. Just as in any practice of Qi Gong, whatever you put into it will be what you get out of it. If you practice for health, you will feel rejuvenated and refreshed. If you aspire to a more cosmic goal, the sky's the limit. The Tao is as large as the infinite universe and as small as the particle with no interior.

When to Practice

Dr. Wu studied the martial arts for years under Wang Sheng Zai, the great martial arts champion. One of his specialties, Hsin I Chuan, is a form of martial arts based on the movements of animals. His training style emphasizes the Tiger Paw; strength, power, and the attack. Therefore, Master Wang would practice his standing posture every day from three to five in the morning, in the hours of the Tiger. At this time, he could most effectively build up the power and strength of the Tiger.

Master Wang confided in Dr. Wu the secret to his outstanding string of competition victories. He would always make sure that at least half the matches would be held between 3 A.M. and 5 A.M.—the hours when he could maximize his potential. His body was acclimatized to those hours due to his daily practice, and because they were the hours of the Tiger, he could best utilize the attack force of the Tiger Paw. He would flip his opponents in two seconds and defend his championship title every time. Also, to register with Master Wang for a fight, his opponents were required to produce their passports. He would take down their birth information and then tell them when he would compete with them based on their birth date, year, and time. Dr. Wu thinks fondly of his teacher as a unique individual who has made a lasting contribution to Chinese martial arts.

This story points out the importance of choosing the right time to practice. To find your animal time, refer to the Animal Hours chart in Chapter 2. Locate your birth time and its corresponding animal hours. This is your best time to do Qi Gong. If, for example, you were born at 4 A.M., you are a Tiger hour person. But if you can't crawl out of bed at the Tiger hours of 3 A.M. to 5 A.M., do your practice between three and five in the afternoon instead. This is the Chinese way of following the flow. Do the practice at the time that is best for you and you will gain the most benefit.

If you were born between three and five in the morning, then this is the best time for you to combine the Yin and Yang forces within you. This brings out your Original Qi. This is the theory of the *Chinese Classic of Internal Medicine*. The person you were born into this world as was created by heaven and earth. The moment you were born, the best part of you was born—the part that is most truly you. Your birth time was perfectly timed, generated by that special blend of Yin and Yang that was meant for you alone. Therefore, practicing according to your birth time will provide you with the best general results.

In specific circumstances, Qi Gong can be practiced at other times of the day. If you're not feeling well or you need to work on a particular organ, traditional Chinese medicine has determined the specific hours of the day to best facilitate healing. Qi Gong practiced at the appropriate organ hour can have a beneficial result. These hours represent the peak functioning of the various organs in the twenty-four-hour cycle. When an organ is working at its highest efficiency, it is easier to send more healing Qi to it. For example, if you want to work on your stomach, practice between 7 A.M. and 9 A.M. Qi Gong at this time will enhance its effect on the stomach more that at any other time. Consult with a doctor of Oriental medicine to determine the perfect hours for your health condition. One exception is the kidney, which can be focused on at five to seven, morning and evening, and along with the stomach, at seven to nine in the morning. Practicing during organ hours is a Yin (internal) practice. The Five Centers Facing Heaven is a Yin form of Qi Gong that absorbs energy from the moon and works on the internal balance of the body. It is a beautiful practice from the White Cloud Monastery that is a subject in itself. However, Qi Gong for Feng Shui trains your energy outwards, which is a Yang practice. Therefore, the Five Mystic Codes and the Golden Steel Unbreakable Body meditations presented in this book should be practiced during your animal hours.

The Five Mystic Codes

The Five Mystic Codes comprise the core training system for Taoist Feng Shui. They are signs between you the universe, and they are at the root of building your Qi. Spending a half-hour or so a day with their practice will open doors of experience that are magical, unexpected, and uniquely yours.

THE HEART SECRET

The purpose of the first Mystic Code, the Heart Secret, is to train yourself to the point that whatever you think, happens. You have to

The Five Mystic Codes

The Heart Secret—turning thought into reality/attaining heart awareness

The Emerging Secret—human and heaven become one/awareness of nature

The Mind Secret—communication with the universal mind/cosmic awareness

The Mouth Secret—five-element incantation/awareness of unity

The Body Secret—turning the vision around to look within/awareness of one's true self

develop a conscious mastery of your powers of thought. This is done using your first thought in the morning. The moment you awaken out of sleep, immediately think the thought that you wish to come true. It must be your very first thought or it will not work. The training is not effective if you open your eyes, let a few random thoughts float through your mind, then realize what you're doing, pull yourself together, and think about what you want to have happen. It will not be accurate and you won't get the benefit of the practice.

This sounds simple enough, but it really is a challenge to maintain, morning after morning. It takes willpower, focus, concentration, and discipline, but by continuing to practice you will naturally strengthen all of these abilities. Further on, you will stimulate the connection between your brain and the ethical nature of your heart. You learn to focus your wishes and send them out.

Here is an example: I have a sick friend. I sincerely wish her to get well. So, the very first thing I think about when I come out of sleep is my friend and making her well. I *see* her get well. The best time to do this is when the birds are singing in the early morning. Sometimes, you may get lazy and sleep into the morning. Do the practice anyway. It is still better than not thinking about it at all. It's better, but not as effective as when the birds are singing. If you want health, strength, or success for yourself, then the first thing you think about should be that. This is very important.

How can you reach the level of making your wishes happen? There is a special practice that must be done the night before. Let's say that tomorrow morning you want to wish someone well. Then, tonight you must practice the Heart Secret with the moon. Between the hours of 7 P.M. and 9 P.M., stand facing the moon. If you can't see the moon, stand in the direction you think it may approximately be, or stand facing south. Relax and stand with your arms down and your feet shoulder-width apart, with your feet pointed slightly inward to open up the pelvis. Your chin should be down to keep the upper spine straight. This is the basic Qi Gong stance.

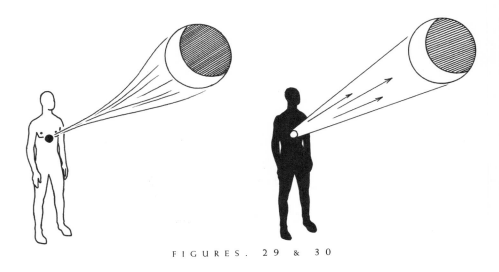

First, you are going to let the moon shine on you. Then, you are going to shine back to the moon. This whole process is visualized through your mind. You have to imagine that your upper body is a moon. Think or feel this in any way it comes naturally to you. Then, have the moon shine down on you and into a special point called the Tan Zhong Shi. This spot is not exactly a part of the physical body, but it is located at a point approximately 2 inches to 2-½ inches down from the midway point between the two nipples. There are a number of English translations of Tan Zhong Shi. *Zhong* means "center," *Shi* means "temple" or "pavilion," and *Tan*, poorly translated as "pond," is a body of water like a small river that seems to be still but is really moving very slowly and gently. Remember, healthy water always circulates. Use this definition of Tan Zhong Shi to help visualize the flow of energy between you and the moon (fig. 29).

Allow the moon to shine into you until you feel energized with a special feeling. Then use the Tan Zhong point to reflect the energy back to the moon (fig. 30). Once you feel a warm sensation, you can stop. This training takes between three and ten minutes—or around five minutes on average. People have said how good they feel after they have done the moon practice. If this is the case for you, you can practice for up to twenty minutes.

Again, first the moon shines on you, and then you reflect back to it. Don't think of your wishes at this time. Don't think about anything. Just experience your sensations with a quiet mind. After you have practiced, relax and go to bed. To do the Heart Secret, you must make a small sacrifice. You're going to have to suffer a little bit. When you go to sleep at night after your practice, don't use any blankets. This is be cause the minute you feel a chill, you will wake up suddenly. This is the moment when you must fix your desired thought in your mind. It must be the first thought that comes into your mind. You can't get up and go to the bathroom and think whatever you want to think. What you want to accomplish has to be in your mind first, before you do any activity.

This is a very powerful discipline. Do not underestimate its ability to create change. Look for the feeling inside you when you face the moon. The loving energy of the moon has the power to dissolve all bad luck and negativity. You can wish for your own personal objectives, for finding a successful career, or for a location with good Feng Shui, for example. You can wish for the welfare of others or for their harm. Be careful. Farmers going out in the morning on slaughtering day will find their animals already kneeling down and crying. If you tell your house plants every day to please grow well, they will grow much better than if you don't say anything, or they will weaken and die if those are your thoughts. If someone has done you harm, watch the first thought that comes into your mind in the morning. If you think this person shouldn't have done their bad deed, strict justice will take its course upon them. You are sending the message. Ultimately, the choice of what to think is up to you. In the Heart Secret, you give a message to the moon, and the moon gives it back.

The heart is like the moon. Practice the Heart Secret and it will soon work; don't and it won't. This may sound very magical, but in reality, it is a natural part of daily life. When I was a little girl, the very first thing I wanted to be was an opera singer. How could I have possibly known at age six that by the time I was in my late teens and my voice matured, I would have nearly a four-octave range without any training? When Dr. Wu was a boy, he always said he would study at Beijing University when he grew up, and that's exactly what he did. How often do we find that our most strongly held convictions come true?

The thoughts in our minds, going as far back as childhood, are messages that are all still out there, held in the cosmic net of the Ling Zi. Remember, we only posses half of our soul in our bodies. The other half is in heaven, guiding our actions. The Ling Qi transmits this guidance. Sometimes, in a sudden flash, parents might have a premonition to get home quickly, where they find their child taken ill. Maybe a bowl drops out of your hands and shatters for no reason. You could just forget about it, but having a Taoist perspective would warn you that something is wrong. By checking the exact time the bowl was broken, you could determine the corresponding events that are being foreshadowed. If you know the *I Ching*, you would immediately look to your trigrams to find the hidden meaning of the incident.

Why is the moon practice so essential? Facing the moon enhances your ability to connect with the Ling Zi. With this practice you are cultivating your ability to bring Qi out from your body so it may carry your questions to the universe. When the Ling up above is able to receive your information, it will then direct you to what you must do down on earth. Taoists have practiced with the moon for 1,700 years, and this is their conclusion. Collect the essence of the moon into your heart, and your first thought in the morning will come true. This may be a difficult concept to accept, but just like playing Mozart to help your plants grow, it works. It works through the Heart Secret Facing the Moon.

There are eight different ways to communicate with the moon. In addition to the Heart Secret, another exercise that works very well for Feng Shui is the Mi Lien, or Mystic Practice. In this case, you shine out to the moon first, then let it shine back to you until you feel heat. Keep practicing until your inner vision is filled with light. Put the image of the house you are looking at into your mind and allow your consciousness to send you its signs.

If you bring the image of the house into focus and it looks like a house, it's a good place. If you can't bring an image of it together or if it appears upside down, the Feng Shui is not good. If you have a question about a certain person, you can put the person's image into your mind in the same way. If the person then appears standing up, he or she is "upright." Again, if the image is upside down or just can't seem to come into focus, this indicates that the person cannot be trusted. The Mystic Practice is traditionally done in the eighth month of the Chinese lunar calendar, the time of the Chinese lunar festival and the time of the harvest moon. During this time of the year, the moon is at its closest point to the earth and exerts its strongest magnetic pull on the waters of the ocean and of our bodies. The Ling Zi is most active now, adding strength to your practice and enhancing the effectiveness of your results.

THE EMERGING SECRET

The second Taoist method of Feng Shui, the Emerging Secret, is known in Chinese as Chu Mi. *Chu* means "going out." This is the practice of human and universe combining as one. To communicate with heaven, the human life force must go out, go up, emerge. You have to meditate.

First, sit straight in a chair or cross-legged on the floor. Three feet above your head, imagine a radiant cloud, its light bluish-purple like an ultraviolet ray. Sit for twenty minutes, breathing naturally (fig. 31).

There is a Taoist saying about meditation:

FIGURE. 31

"Zuo Huang Ru Jin Ru Di." *Zuo Huang* means sitting still, breathing naturally. *Ru Jin* means not thinking of anything. You are very calm. *Ru Di* is the point at which your concentration becomes so deep that no outside distractions can enter in. You wouldn't hear someone call your name. You have forgotten yourself. Your whole body and the environment mix together, united as one. Your body might even feel like an egg. It is at this point that you feel the bluish-purple cloud above your head.

The most common image of God is of an all-knowing being in the sky above our heads, watching over us. This is also the principle of the Emerging Secret. It's like trying to build a mountain, pebble by pebble. Pile up all the dirt and soon there will stand a lofty mountain gathering bright rain clouds above its peak. Your head is also a mountain. The space above your eyebrows is your heaven. This is how you connect with the clouds.

Meditating with the purple cloud trains your head to sense Qi. The head is basically all Yang Qi. When the Qi has completely left the head, a person is at that point considered dead. The hands and feet of a corpse feel cold, but actually the head feels colder. When he worked the emergency ward, Dr. Wu would check to see if patients were still alive by putting his hand on their heads.

In Feng Shui, we try to use the Yang of our heads to match up with the Yang of the heavens. The first thing to do when taking a Feng Shui reading is to look upward. When we look up, our heads naturally seek out the Qi. Taoists believe the sign of a successful person is the tilt of his or her head. Especially in women, when you see their heads held high as they walk, you know they are successful in their careers. Madeleine Albright, Hillary Rodham Clinton, and Margaret Thatcher all have that upward tilt. Seeing someone with his or her head hanging down all the time is self-explanatory. When people come to see Dr. Wu to find out whether they are going to be successful or not, and they have their head held down, Dr. Wu already knows. He usually tells them, "How about instead of a fortune, you come in for a treatment to fix your neck?" With your head up, you collect good Qi; with your head down, you waste it.

The purpose of the Emerging Secret meditation is to strengthen your ability, when you look up, to target the Qi with the Yang channels in your head (fig. 32). With daily practice, you will reach a certain level where, when you read the Feng Shui, you will feel a special sensation above your head. When you walk into a place and you have a warm, comfortable sensation, then it's a good place. If you feel coldness above your head, there is not enough Qi in that spot.

FIGURE. 32

You can strengthen your Yang Qi to the point where even in windy or overcast conditions, it can penetrate straight through the interference to observe the clouds. An indication of a kidney disorder is sudden shaking or quivering upon urination. A Taoist method of treating this problem is to clench your teeth when you go to the bathroom. This can help to preserve your kidneys. Similarly, if you walk into a place and your head starts to quiver, watch out. There is a lack of Yang Qi overhead. This is a natural reaction of your newly developed senses. As an added bonus, visualizing the purple cloud will help fortify your kidneys. Of course, not everyone can reach the level of mastery of a professional Feng Shui practitioner. But with sincere and regular practice, anyone can learn how to help themselves and their loved ones.

THE MIND SECRET

The Emerging Secret is the act of the human reaching out to combine with the universe. In turn, the Mind Secret is the universe flowing inward to combine with the human. In Mind Secret meditation, then, you try to concentrate the Qi from the universe down into your body.

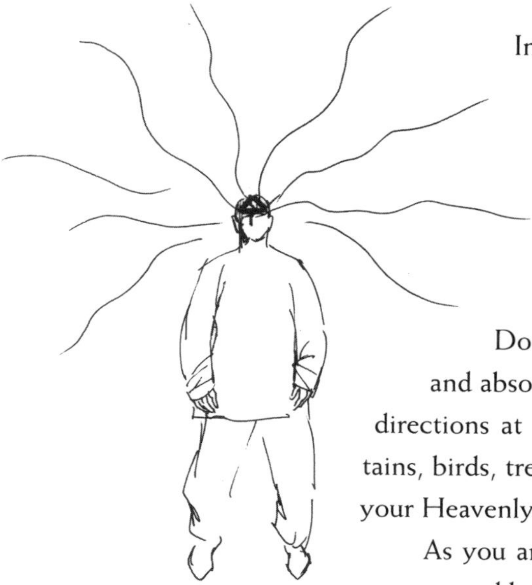

In a sitting or standing position, relax and breathe gently and regularly. It's easy to hold your breath in this meditation, so be aware and keep your breathing flowing. Gather the Qi from the universe. Draw it in and place it in your Upper Dan. Don't release it. Just keep drawing it in and absorbing it. Collect the Qi from all four directions at once. Don't think about the mountains, birds, trees, or flowers. Just let their Qi enter your Heavenly Eye (fig. 33).

FIGURE. 33

As you are looking at a location, stand at its center and bring all its Qi into your body. Hold it in for thirty to sixty seconds. If your body starts to feel comfortable or warm, then this is a good place for you. If you feel cold, it's not a good place. Also, if after you gather the Qi you find you have a headache, then the place is bad for you. Don't move in. Use this practice when gauging the Qi of a place for yourself personally. Checking the Qi for others involves another procedure that is discussed later in this chapter.

You can use the Mind Secret to find the places and even the people that suit you best. Dr. Wu recently interviewed a woman for a position at his clinic. Her clerical experience was excellent and her English was as fluent as her Chinese, but Dr. Wu knew he couldn't hire her. While they were talking, Dr. Wu did the Mind Secret practice. He wound up with a splitting headache for the rest of the afternoon. Now, you might feel sorry for this woman, but when two people's Qi do not mesh, it can cause serious problems for the both of them. With this technique, you can avoid unnecessary problems and dangers altogether. Be forewarned: If, as you are gathering the Qi, you start feeling any discomfort, do not allow it in. Consider yourself fortunate to have averted still greater trouble from your life.

Taoist Feng Shui is not based solely on what surrounds you. You can put a plant here and a wind chime there, but since neither is a part of the Original Qi, it cannot change what has been there from the beginning. By arranging things properly around your house you may ameliorate the problem, but you won't get to its root. By using the Mind Secret method, you can actually change the Qi, making it good for you. When you do this practice, you are exchanging messages with the universe. Just as you can bring these messages in, so you can send them out again.

Dr. Wu has a patient whose father lives in New York. Her father has cancer and has suffered a heart attack. She comes once a week to Dr. Wu's clinic. Meanwhile, in New York, the father is in the hospital being monitored by his doctors. Dr. Wu has her lay down with her father's picture placed on her body. First, he focuses his mind on her. Then, superimposed on her image, he concentrates on the image of her father. This sends a message out. Immediately after this treatment, the father's vital signs improve. Right now, her father is experiencing a general recovery from both his cancer and his heart attack, and all his test results are on record. You might think this unscientific or unbelievable, but for the Taoists, it is a highly researched and developed system that is based on the power of the mind's pulsations.

Dr. Wu first realized the importance of these brain impulses when he was a young man. He was with some of his college friends on a vacation. One night in the hotel, his friend woke up in the middle of the night, jumped out of bed, and started hurriedly putting on his clothes. He said he knew his father was at the train station and he had to find him quickly. Dr. Wu and the others got up and followed their friend to make sure he didn't get lost or hurt in his sudden urgency. When they reached the train station, they found the student's father there. He was lost, not knowing at which hotel to find his son. At that moment, Dr. Wu realized the full importance of the Mind Secret.

The father had come for his son because of a major family crisis. But when he got off the train, he realized that he had no idea which hotel his son was staying at, and he became very nervous and anxious. Although the son was asleep, he still received the message of his father's mind. Since this time, Dr. Wu has researched and conducted experiments on the power of the brain's ability to send a current through the universal mind and out to those it must reach. He has connected with loved ones and treated patients with this technique by putting them into his mind. Some things are understood only by the way we are willing to look at them. Try it yourself and see how it works.

There is an important ethical aspect of the Heart and Mind Secret practices. To see your wishes in your mind and make them come true, you have to be right minded. Do good things for others without expecting a return. Having a good heart is the road to achieving what your heart desires. It's a cycle that increases upon itself. If you are always upstanding and helpful to the people around you, they will think of you as a good person. Their belief in you and their reliance on you will, in turn, create more opportunities for you to do good. You will feel a sense of accomplishment, and before you know it, your spiritual foundation will be built up.

Even if you don't have many opportunities to help others directly, you can still develop your ethical nature by practicing Qi Gong. When you do the standing postures with sincerity, you are helping the planet. Trees absorb energy from the sun and release oxygen into the atmosphere. By doing Qi Gong, you accomplish the same thing. You take universal Qi into your body, and then your own spiritual energy radiates out. In the martial arts and Qi Gong, sometimes just standing still accomplishes more than a lot of movement. Practicing well, you spread your Qi out through the environment. You are doing a good deed for the earth. Being a righteous person, you will achieve your goals.

THE MOUTH SECRET

The fourth of the Mystic Codes is the Mouth Secret. There are many different methods of prayer. The Mouth Secret uses sound to send out messages. It is based on six syllables known as the "Greater

Enlightenment Six Character Words of Truth," forming a pow mantra that harmonizes the emotions.

Repeat the following six words out loud to yourself after you have finished practicing the Mind Secret or at any time of the day when you wish to gain more composure, grounding, or courage: Om-Ma-Ni-Ma-Om-Yo. This is the transliteration from the Sanskrit. You can also use the Taoist version of the phrase: Bu Tan Tsai, Bu Shi Mi.

All his life, Lao Tze said these six words. Whether said in Sanskrit or Chinese, they carry the same meaning. Taoists interpret them to mean, "I am not greedy; I am not afraid of death." Greed does not simply mean wanting more money. Lusting after results of any kind is the basis of much of our problems. Without greed there are no problems. There is no reason to worry. All our troubles and anxieties exist because we are all too greedy. The fear of death is what leads us straight to it. If you are not worried for your health, you won't become sick. When bad luck and misfortune know you are not afraid of living or dying, they won't bother to come to you. The greater your fear, the more you strengthen the thought vibration that can pull sickness into your life.

Keeping your mind clear of worry and fear is an important prerequisite for any deep spiritual practice. This does not mean becoming apathetic or blank. The feeling that every day just blends into the next and that we are just along for the ride is just as much an illusion as is fear. We are all here for a reason. Never give up your power. You might ask, why not just recite the Mouth Secret first, before starting the meditations? The symbolism of practicing the Heart, Emerging, and Mind Secrets before saying the Mouth Secret prayer stresses the necessity of first finding the true purpose of your heart, spirit, and mind. Only then do we ascend to greater levels of clarity. Only at this point can we accept the full power of the Mouth Secret to aid us on our way. The Mouth Secret is an incantation that marshals to our aid all of our inner forces. By uniting the Five Elements, we can receive the Tao.

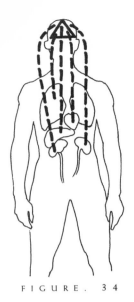

FIGURE. 34

Looking back over the first four stages of the Mystic Codes, we have first connected our heart to the forces of the universe, then our heads, our thoughts, and finally our emotions. Now we are ready to look within. This is called the Shen Mi, or the Body Secret. We have already absorbed all the Qi from around us into the Upper Dan during the Mind Secret meditation. Now, turning our vision inward, we want to try and send all this Qi down through our bodies.

With your eyes closed, use the Qi to look inside of yourself. Try to see down inside of your body, visualizing your internal organs one by one (fig. 34). Look at yourself and figure yourself out. Understand what is inside of you. The code of the *Art of War* states that to do battle, you must know yourself first in order to know your opponent. This will lead you to success. You will be unable to be defeated. Understanding yourself completely will help you understand any situation you will encounter.

This has many applications for Feng Shui. You know that if you take your troops into a forest, you will have to take precautions to prevent the enemy from setting it on fire. The same thing holds true if you move to an area where brushfires are common. Before you decide on a house, survey the surrounding terrain for dry scrub and other possible pathways fire might take toward the property. Determine your potential escape routes. Knowing this information in advance will help you pick a house that is as safe and secure as you require.

When Dr. Wu's clinic was in a previous location, he could tell right away from its Feng Shui that its disadvantages included not being able to stay there indefinitely. Its advantages outweighed its disadvantages, though, so he made sure to take precautions before he moved in. Because of the adjustments he made, he was able to stay there and grow his practice, while all the other units in the building changed hands many times over.

Using the Qi to look inside of yourself is a very profound practice for maintaining your health. Look inside with your eyes closed, moving the Qi from your head down to your toes, observing each organ and noting all the sensations or impressions you receive. If the Qi stops or becomes blocked, that indicates a potential health problem. For example, if you are casting your gaze down through your body and it stops at your liver, try to concentrate and move it further through. If you still can't see past it, then you know that today there is something wrong with your liver. If it's windy outside, then you know not to go out that day. Wind is harmful to the liver. If instead you see no problem with the liver but do see a joint problem, it's a good day to go out. Wind can ease arthritic pains.

It's not difficult to see how this practice can be easily transferred for a Feng Shui application. If you look within and know what health problems you have, you can go about picking a living environment that will help to care for your condition. So, if it's a liver disorder, you know not to choose a very windy place. In fact, a location with too much wind is never good. While mild breezes will bring money, harsh winds will make you lose your fortune. However, if you know you have issues with your liver, you will also know to be extra careful about winds and drafts. In this situation, even a mild wind might not be appropriate.

Another important point to note about the Body Secret is that if you do see a problem, the chances are very likely you have caught it well in advance. Using Qi to see, one observes things on a level interior to the simple physical plane. Consult with or have yourself evaluated by a Western or an Eastern medical practitioner. You may well be able to prevent a serious illness before it has the chance to manifest itself outwardly. As mentioned earlier, the practice of Qi Gong has the ability to change your body on a deep, cellular level.

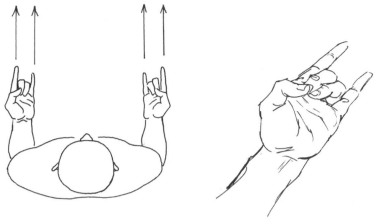

Hand Seals

To complete your practice of the Five Mystic Codes, you may make special hand signals to break with the circle of energy you have created. In Taoist Feng Shui methodology, these mudras can also be used to check a house's energy. Although there are three special hand seals, only two of them are used for Yang houses (houses of the living). The third hand seal is used for checking Yin conditions in underground tombs and graves, and as such it is beyond the scope of this book.

When you see someone with hands together in prayer, the hand's posture is a signal of salute. One hand up to the face is a signal of polite courtesy. The first of the two Taoist mudras is meant to bring safety and peace and to avoid misfortune (fig. 35). If you read the Qi of a house with this hand seal, nothing there will be able to harm you. With your elbows bent and your forearms held straight in front of you, place your hands palm up. Form a circle with your thumb by placing it over your second and ring fingers. Point your index fingers and pinkies straight out. This position will check for problems. You can even execute this hand signal when your child is crying. It will tell you why he or she is crying. Dr. Wu had a neighbor whose infant would cry loudly every night for an extended period of time. Dr. Wu did this seal back and forth across the baby's back, and after he did so, the child would be fine.

Remember, this hand seal brings peace and security. It can also help you pinpoint the source of any bad Qi in your home. First, absorb the Qi; then walk through your house. When you start to feel any unusual sensations in your fingers, you know you are getting warm. The closer you get to the source of the bad Qi, the more obvious the sensations will be.

Dr. Wu once did the Feng Shui for a prominent family's very large home. The family was feeling scared and oppressed. An uneasy feeling seemed to pervade the entire house. A previous Feng Shui practitioner had put grains of rice all over the house and had even sacrificed a chicken in one of the rooms. None of this had done any good. When Dr. Wu first entered the home, he thought to himself, "What the heck is this?" The rooms were full of rice and covered in chicken blood. No wonder the family was terrified. As Dr. Wu walked around the house, he stopped in a room where a large Qing Dynasty porcelain vase was standing in a corner. When he approached and checked the vase with this hand seal, his hands started to feel as if they had been hurt or injured. He turned the vase around and saw that it had a hairline crack running diagonally across the painted decoration of a lady. The crack ran right through her face. The owners had turned the cracked side of the vase toward the wall to hide the damage. He told them to either fix the crack or move the vase outside. To repair the costly antique properly would require shipping it back to Taiwan or China, so they just put it out on the porch. Now their house feels fine. This is a very important mudra. Put the Qi into your hands and then test it.

If you don't get results with the first hand seal, which is for blessing the Qi, you may use the second one (fig. 36). Your hands are held in front

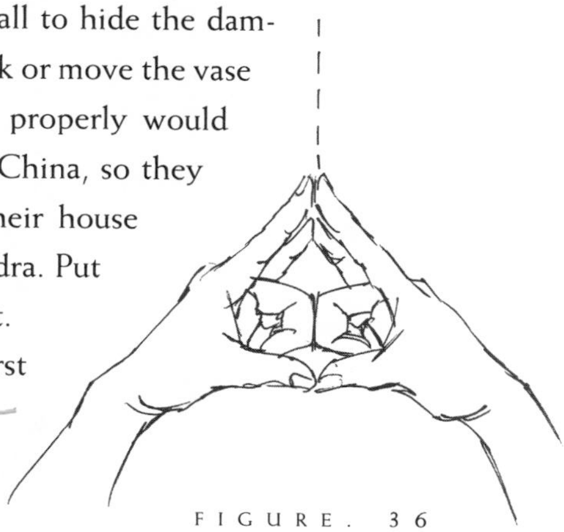

FIGURE. 36

of your chest, with the forefingers and pinkies touching at their tips—as when you play "Here's the church, here's the steeple"—but pointing outward instead of upward. Meanwhile, the second and ring fingers curl down to touch from the first to the second knuckles with their tips resting on the thumbs, whose tips also touch, forming a small triangular space in the center. This hand seal is for detecting and resolving difficult Qi. Once your hands are in this position, concentrate on making whatever unpleasant feeling you are sensing dissolve away.

Another house Dr. Wu looked at had a very unsettling feeling. Already it had changed owners three times, and the current residents were noticing weird occurrences, as if a poltergeist was present. Using the first hand seal, Dr. Wu detected that there were some souls in the house. He talked with them and they communicated back that they didn't want to leave the house. But when he used the second hand seal, they had no choice but to withdraw.

It is very important to be aware of the possibility, in the serious practice of Qi Gong or Feng Shui, of making definite contact with entities from other planes. You may encounter some situations that are so obvious that the issue is no longer a question of believing or disbelieving. When you begin to open your perceptions to the universal Qi, becoming aware of forms of life that your newly refined senses can perceive is a common experience. Just remember that you never need to be afraid of these energies. Always know that as a living human being equipped with the power of free will and kindness in your heart, you will always be more capable than these entities. Simply communicate with them in a nonjudgmental manner, as you would with a plant or an animal. You may discover some remarkable things. It is true that these encounters can be unnerving, due to their disconnection from everything commonly held to be "normal" and "human." Actually, it is a great blessing for you and these forces to be in contact with each other. By doing Feng Shui and Qi Gong, you will actually be assisting them to finally be at peace, while also helping your family and friends.

Doing these practices with diligence can develop unusual abilities to communicate with energy at many different levels. Taoists believe that to master these arts, you have to be chosen from heaven. Personally, I believe that most people have some innate potential to unfold these untapped powers of the mind. However, these powers become meaningless tricks, like being able to rollerblade backward on one foot, if they are not put to the service of helping others. A selfless heart is the first and foremost requirement of a Taoist Feng Shui master.

5

The Secret of the
Unbreakable Body

With this chapter, we enter the inner-circle mysteries of the
Taoist Feng Shui masters. Dr. Wu has waited thirteen years
for the right time to reveal these secret practices publicly, on the wish
of his master. They are at once absolutely simple and supremely profound. We have to indicate at this point that these practices must be
used strictly for personal self-exploration and helping one's close family
and friends. They are not meant to replace certified medical care or
to be used for the professional practice of Feng Shui. These techniques

tend to raise more questions than they answer; therefore, we recommend that readers who desire serious training seek to study under the careful eye of a true teacher.

There are two types of spiritual energy in the universe. Ling Wen refers to the human soul. Ling Qi is the spiritual energy belonging to all other creatures. The *Ancient Book of Lu* says even a blade of grass or a clump of dirt has Ling Qi. As a Feng Shui practitioner, you cannot simply be alert to the Ling of your surroundings. You must also cultivate yourself to bring out this Ling from your own body, so that you can communicate with your environment. If you don't cultivate yourself to bring out your Ling energy, you are just a normal person. You won't be able to feel the plants, the clouds, the soil. You won't be capable of receiving the messages they are trying to give you.

Dr. Wu firmly believes that in order to be a true Feng Shui master, not only do you have to be aware of your surroundings, you also have to train yourself to project this Ling from your body. This is the essence of making contact with the world around you. You wouldn't deserve to be called a Feng Shui master if you didn't cultivate your Ling and your Qi. Dr. Wu has been approached by many Western Feng Shui practitioners, but when he talks to them he sees that all they have been taught are the rudimentary facts. Even many so-called Feng Shui masters from China do not practice cultivation. All their information has been learned only on an intellectual level. This isn't enough. Feng Shui has many difficult theories and methods to learn. Not all of them can be grasped with the intellect alone. It's simply not as easy as gathering information from a few books.

Dr. Wu has been asked many times to teach Feng Shui classes and seminars, but he feels this is just not his cup of tea. The way he sees it, learning the alphabet is easy. You can memorize the letters *A* to *Z* in a moment's time. But whether you can use the twenty-six letters to write an interesting article is quite another thing. Unless you pass many years in practice, it will be very difficult to do. We all speak and understand English. Whether we are able to express serious ideas gracefully or are completely inarticulate is what makes the difference.

Jin Gan Bu Huai

How do you cultivate Ling energy? First, you must begin by cultivating the Qi of your body. Your body's Qi is the most important thing to train. Remember, in the Tao, no Qi equals no Tao. Dr. Wu estimates that 90 percent of those who call themselves Qi Gong masters have read a lot of books but have not cultivated their own Qi. Ultimately, all the books in the world will not increase or strengthen your Qi. Doing so takes physical practice.

If a person's Qi is weak, he or she cannot go out and read Feng Shui for other people. Feng Shui practitioners who look weak—with sallow skin, gaunt cheekbones, and little vitality of spirit—need to take care of themselves first, not busy themselves with trying to make money off of others. Would you trust a surgeon with heart disease and high blood pressure to operate on your body? Dr. Wu's basic advice for finding a Qi Gong master or a Feng Shui practitioner is this: If the person looks tired, is yawning a lot, or can't walk, look for someone else because this one won't do you any good.

How, then, do you train your body's Qi? You need to practice until your body radiates light. Many different religions portray their masters as people encircled by light. Anyone can cultivate this light. Every single one of us has light. This light not only enhances the physical body. It is your communication with the universe as well. This light is your protection from evil and a powerful force for good.

Dr. Wu has known doctors who had very little actual book learning but are able to cure whoever comes to them. Why? Because their ethics and their goodness are protecting them. When they "treat" patients, it's really the sharing of their inner goodness that provides the cure. The same thing holds true for the practice of the martial arts. If you also possess ethics deep inside of yourself, every day when you practice, you are not only building your martial arts skill, you are also practicing your ethics. The training of your ethical nature is more important than your postures or movements. When Dr. Wu's teacher practiced T'ai Chi, he would often stand in a single stance for hours. Sometimes you have to come to a certain degree of understanding to comprehend the full implications of this great truth.

The Taoist adept of the Tang Dynasty, Lu Dongbin, wrote an extensive treatise on this subject. In it he discusses how to cultivate yourself, bring your goodness out, and be an ethical person. The point is to nourish and develop your heart and mind, your kindness and strength. If there is peace within your heart and your mind, the whole world will be peaceful. This is called the Xin Gong, or the Heart Practice. Through Qi cultivation, you bring out the light around you. Your body then becomes like gold and steel—unbreakable, invincible, all-protected. You cannot be defeated.

Jin Gan Bu Huai, or the Golden Steel Unbreakable Body, is the name of the practice that creates this indestructible shield. *Jin* means "gold," *Gan* "steel," and *Bu Huai* "cannot break." All the forms of Qi Gong that Dr. Wu teaches lead gradually to this strength filled with light, but this particular technique leads directly to this result. Diligent nightly practice will bring you swiftly to its attainment.

First, stand relaxed with your feet shoulder width-apart in the basic Qi Gong stance. The next step is to open all the pores. When Dr. Wu does Feng Shui, he shields his body with the Jin Gan Bu Huai practice. Incoming and outgoing energy, Yin and Yang, are the basic concepts behind this technique. The teachings of Sakyamuni Buddha state that the hair follicles of the body consist of 84,000 *Fa Men*, or Dharma Gates, and 84,000 *Gui Men*, or Ghost Gates, connected together in pairs. *Fa* is defined by Taoists as the way of resolving things for the good. The Fa Gates work like talismanic controls and are directed by the heart's focus. The evil inclination is also controlled by the heart.

The dark ghosts of the Gui Men reside inside all of us. The object of this practice is to shoot all the ghosts and negative energy out of our bodies. With this, you will open the Fa, or Dharma, inside of your heart. These gates find their physical expression in the inhalations and exhalations of your body's pores, but to conduct this process from within, you must let it come from the heart.

Don't worry about all this talk of ghosts. Remember, humans are the highest order of creation. Our essence is superior to all others in nature. In the Six Realms, humans are on the top. Even the trees and animals try to cultivate themselves. Still, no matter what they do, they will remain on a level lower than that of a cultivated human being.

After standing and relaxing, gradually empty out the inside of your body. All of your organs should feel hollow inside. The lungs are empty, the intestines are empty, the lower torso is empty. Every part of you is hollow. Even your head is empty. Your whole body is a hollow shell. Let Fa pass through your mind. You are empty and hollow. One

The Golden Steel Unbreakable Body Health Practice

1. Stand with your feet shoulder-width apart and relax.
2. Let your body become empty in this order.
   1. Chest
   2. Abdomen
   3. Lower torso and legs
   4. Arms
   5. Head

   Feel as though you have dissected yourself.
3. Feel yourself become a solid, unbreakable object: mountain, gold, steel.
4. Go to sleep, as you continue to feel solid and strong.

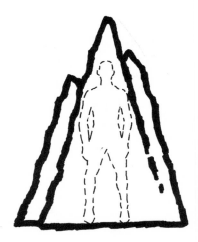

FIGURE. 3 7

by one, let your chest become hollow, then your abdomen, your legs, your arms, and, finally, your skull. After you clear out your body, it contains only these five hollow areas. You have become invisible. You cease to exist. Your physical body is gone. You have dissected yourself, dissolved and given your body back to nature. This process comes from the mind. This is how the Taoists and Buddhists cultivate themselves to achieve and become Jin Gan Bu Huai.

Every night before you go to bed, do this practice of emptying the self. After you become perfectly hollow, imagine yourself becoming the most solid, unbreakable thing you can conceive of. What is the strongest? Use your mind to become a mountain, a piece of gold, a block of steel, even a diamond (fig. 37). While you hold this feeling within your mind and your body, allow yourself to drift off to sleep. Don't assume that "Golden Steel Unbreakable Body" is just a quaint saying. As you practice, day by day, night by night, your body will become this mountain, just as strong as gold and steel. You will find that you don't get sick as often. You may get to the point where you won't even need a blanket to sleep at night. This is a fundamental Taoist practice. It is the foremost method of Unbreakable Body Health.

Qi Practice

The emptying and strengthening process of Jin Gan Bu Huai is crucial for Qi Gong cultivation. The whole reason for practicing Qi Gong is to turn your body into a vessel that all the energy of the universe can flow through. When you can think yourself hollow, becoming an empty container, then you are ready to let things come in and store them away. A study hall must be empty for people to come in and have a class. A house must be empty before you can move in. My cup must be empty to fill it with water. When we discuss the concept of emptiness, it is not something void and black. The emptiness we seek is a functional emptiness. It must be useful. In making the physical body disappear, it has been given as a gift back to nature. Once you give it all, you gain it all.

Whenever a topic is discussed in the Tao, it always has two sides. Going in one direction automatically gets you to the other side. If you persist in thinking how successful you are—content but oblivious to potential obstacles—eventually you will fail. When the crash comes, you might not even know what hit you. You would have been better off thinking you were a failure the whole time. If instead you prepare yourself for the worst-case scenario, while still working toward the ideal scenario, you will certainly be a success. In every aspect of Taoist study—from the martial arts to reading the Sutras to doing Feng Shui—this is the basic training.

Master Du once said, "Having power, having money—there's no use to it." If you have studied a martial art for so many years that you've forgotten everything your master taught you, only then have you gained the ultimate level of skill. This means after you have learned all you've learned, you utilize it to benefit the best part of you. Parroting a lesson year after year perfectly by heart, always repeating it exactly the same way, is not the highest level of knowledge or understanding. The highest level is achieved when you have so completely assimilated all you have learned that you naturally push past all of it to create something completely new. At this point, your higher self has grown. This is true success.

To discuss another facet of this same idea, your whole body is a martial art. Head, arms, and feet are all weapons. One night, Dr. Wu's three-year-old son jumped up from out of nowhere and bit his fifteen-year-old brother on the ear. Dr. Wu was very pleased. The three-year-old was so small, but he instinctively knew how to fight back. He used the element of surprise and went straight for a sensitive point that he could handle despite the size difference. This is the Taoist way of positive thinking. The *I Ching* trigrams are always changing because we are always changing. The key is to find a pattern for yourself in this kaleidoscope of shifting situations. If you can extract the rhythm or sequence out from of all the changes, then you've got it figured out. You hold the key in your hand.

Taoist Exorcism

The basic Jin Gan Bu Huai practice we have discussed should be done every night before you go sleep. When practiced seriously, it will provide your body with the strength and robust health necessary for the more intricate Qi Gong method required for analyzing Feng Shui or treating sickness. The disciplines of solar and lunar Qi Gong are separate from the method presented in this book. Their primary purpose is self-cultivation and contact with the higher energies of the cosmos. They are exercises that can be done in a daily, general manner. The Five Mystic Codes can also be practiced in this way.

What we will now present is a highly specialized form of Qi Gong in which the practitioner opens the Fa Gates, activates the body's internal radar system, creates a sacred circle, and then calls up, from the force of his or her own body, all the ghosts, evils, and disease of a location or a patient. Then, using the power of the mind, the practitioner removes the sickness, either by pushing it outside its sphere of influence or by capturing and transforming it from within.

The easiest way to describe this entire process is to call it an exorcism. Unfortunately, *exorcism* has the connotation of a desperate battle between powerful evil forces and weak humans who can barely keep from being overwhelmed, as well as images of howling, blood and guts, and violence. As we will see, however, this process is actually a very gentle procedure—firm but loving—that is accomplished in a clear and exalted state of mind. It is a method of communication between living people and the forces of the universe that may not at that time belong with the living. In fact, at times it is more desirable to keep them where they are so they may help instead of harm. The greatest harm comes from what we fear. Awareness wipes away fear and brings wisdom. This ancient rite of practical Taoist spirituality brings that awareness.

Preparation

As in any Qi Gong practice, begin by standing relaxed, with your feet shoulder-width apart. Empty your body as in the basic Jin Gan Bu Huai method—first the chest, then the abdomen, legs, arms, and head, in that order. Inhale gently, slowly, and silently through the nose, filling your chest with air but without straining or clenching the breath. When breathing in Qi Gong, you want everything to be soft and natural. If you are faced with a choice between taking in less air or straining and holding your breath, always take in less breath and stay relaxed. Sometimes during these breathing exercises, holding or stuffing in the breath can result in quite an interesting head rush or vibrating feeling, but this is not the object of the practice. Keep it simple and stay within you body's limits, and you will maximize the flow of Qi through your system, while steadily increasing suppleness and lung capacity.

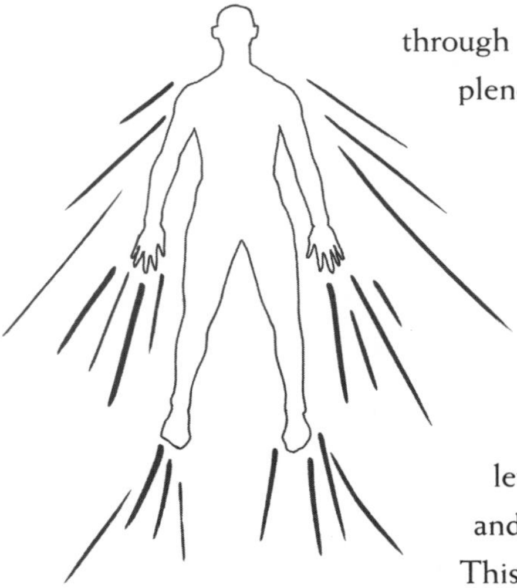

Inhale steadily through the nose and place the Qi in your lower Dan Tian. You can actually swallow the Qi down, if that helps, but remember, clenching is not good. Ideally, it will just flow down gently, put there by your focus. Exhale silently and thinly through the mouth and let the Qi leave through the legs and arms and out the fingers, toes, and soles of the feet. This is how you open all of your Fa Gates (fig. 38). There are no set number of times to repeat this breathing pattern. Just continue inhaling, exhaling, and releasing until you feel relaxed. Sometimes, just from opening the Fa Gates, you can get a clear reading of the situation at hand: the fate of a country, how long a store might be in business, whether a person will live or die.

FIGURE. 38

Next, after breathing and relaxing, you are going to open up your body's communication channels to the universe. The perineum is your starting point. The perineum, the muscle mass that makes up the pelvic floor, is located between the anus and the testicles or vagina. From the center of the perineum, bring the Qi up to the navel. Then take it back and through to the Ming Men or Gates of Life, located directly in line with the navel on the spine. Bring the Qi down and back under, then return to the navel. Repeat thirty-six or seventy-two times, ending at the navel each time. This is done with the mind and does not need to be synchronized with your breathing, which should remain gentle and regular (fig. 39).

From the navel, circle the Qi around the waist to the Ming Men point and then back to the navel. Either direction is fine, but use one direction only. This horizontal circling is done from twelve to thirty-six times, no more or less. This process helps you make special communications with the universe through the human body's natural radar system. After you have circled the Qi, your lower body will begin to breath. This is a very important and powerful type of breathing (fig. 40).

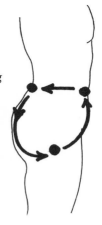

Next, inhale through the nose in three quick, quiet sniffs. Remember, if your sniffs sound loud, somewhere your nostrils or nasal passages are pinching to amplify the sound. You can actually get the air farther into your system if you don't obstruct it or force it through. After the three inhalations, do one short and round exhalation through the mouth accompanied by a quiet, aspirated "ha" sound. Repeat this breathing pattern—three inhales through the nose, one exhale through the mouth— nine times. At this point, most of your hollow body is going to feel hot, especially your chest and arms but the rest of your body will also feel a sensation of heat. This means you are bringing the light forth from your body. You can't always see this light, but you can always feel its heat. When you feel the heat, you have the light. Just like rubbing your feet on the carpet and then touching a doorknob to produce an electrical spark, by using the Qi you accomplish the same thing with your bioelectric energy.

FIGURES.
39 & 40

After you have done the breathing and you feel the heat, you are going to create a circle for yourself. No matter where you are standing—outside in the backyard or in a square or rectangular room—use your eyesight combined with your imagination to see its circular form. Turn it into a circular space and find it's center; then step back, two, three, or five steps, and position yourself in a spot you've left for yourself on its rim. This is the concept of Yu Wei, or standing to the side. The famous Echo Wall in Beijing operates on this principle. If you

stand facing the wall and speak to a friend who is also standing by the wall, your friend will be able to understand every word at every point anywhere along the length of the wall. You may be standing at the far corner, but your voice will echo to any part.

Everything has a center. Stepping back two, three, or five steps from the center to the rim forms a talisman that defines the space for the ritual. Never back up only one step. This invokes a different talisman. When Dr. Wu comes to do Feng Shui, he takes stock of the situation, looks at each person's energy, and then knows where he should stand.

When Dr. Wu taught a group of his students this practice, all of us were standing together in the middle of a courtyard. We did physically take our steps back, but we didn't need to go running to the edge of the courtyard. This process is primarily done in the mind. At a certain level of accomplishment, one doesn't even need to be present in the space to know its Feng Shui. Dr. Wu's teacher, Master Du, could sit in his hall in the White Cloud Monastery and tell what was going on a

FIGURES. 42, 43, & 44

thousand miles away. This is the power of Feng Shui. Remember, as long as you have the circle in your mind, you can easily do the rest of the practice.

Once you have decided where to stand and have taken your two, three, or five steps back, you are going to make your body like the water that ripples out in rings when you throw a stone in its center. Stand with your hands out in front of your body, as if you are holding a huge urn (fig. 41). If you are doing the Feng Shui for a single-storied house, your hands should be at chest level. For a high-rise building, put your hands up high (fig. 42). If it's a basement below street level, hold them down low, palms up (fig. 43). If you're checking the house behind you, put your hands, palm up, to the back (fig. 44). No matter where your hands are, everything in your mind is a circle.

Shake and vibrate your body, bouncing slightly on the balls of your feet as you make the circle larger. From this, rings of wavelike energy expand out from your body. At this point, you are energizing and enhancing the heat and light of your body. Shake and vibrate it outward as far and as high as you can, to the edge of the universe. By doing this, all the Ling of the area will come out and all of its spirits, souls, ghosts, and impurities will arise. The vibrating wave will bring them out. There is no entity you cannot get to appear. This is the central practice of Zheng Yi Sect exorcism. This is how it is actually done by the initiates. It's a very simple technique, but you must practice to master it.

Releasing the Spirits

Now that all of the entities have been brought out, what do you do with them? Use the number 3. As you are shaking, your circular energy reaches out to the edge of the universe. Now, take all the spirits, rocks, and trees that have come out into your consciousness and place them 3 feet, 3 yards, 3 meters, 3 miles—any distance of three—outside of your circle (fig. 45). Actually, each different type of entity has its own distance out. In fact, there are eighteen different levels. For example, if you see a human, put it closest to the 3 measured mark. Evil forces and

FIGURE. 45

ghosts go outside the human level. Trees and rocks go further out still. These are the most common things that may pop up and the three main levels. It all depends on what you have shaken out.

If after you've bounced your energy out, you don't see anything but you know your property has a problem area—a pool, for instance—you can just visualize the pool and put it outside of your circle. If you have real trouble bringing visual images into your inner mind, you may have a problem with your lungs or your liver. Put a tiger (for your lungs) or a dragon (for your liver) outside of your circle. If you bounce and a beautiful woman or handsome man appears to you, this means you will soon have the opportunity for a love affair. It's up to you to decide if you want one or not. If you do, dissolve a part of your shield and let your lover come in. He or she will be yours. Bounce away the bad, let the good come in. This is the Taoist way of thinking.

Once you've bounced all the bad things out past the perimeter of your circle, you will have to put the strength of your shield to the test. Can you control all these ghosts and wild animals and knives from coming through your circle? You have to be strong and firm with yourself. You cannot let any of these things penetrate the shield you have built up around yourself. Test to see if you can hold them back for three to five minutes. At the same time, you want to try and shrink them until they disappear and go away. After you have succeeded in shaking them out and getting rid of them, you have purified your space and have turned misfortune into good luck.

This process can be used for purposes other that reading Feng Shui. With this Qi Gong method, you can discover anything from the fate of a nation to how long a store might stay in business. Simply focus on your question, whether large or small, vibrate your body, and see what comes out in your mind's eye. This Qi Gong process can also protect you from attackers. Dr. Wu was held at gunpoint by three assailants one night while on his way to the supermarket. He just started doing this bouncing and they ran away. Maybe they had no idea what he was going to do next, or maybe it was the energy that chased them away.

Personally, I have reason to believe it was the energy. A number of years ago, I was attacked by a man with a knife. Though it was before Dr. Wu taught me this particular method, I thought to myself, "Okay, if this is it, I want to go out in the best way I can." I focused my mind to the most spiritually elevated plane that I could muster, until I felt swept up in a surge of radiant light. Wouldn't you know it? The knife didn't go in. The assailant aimed straight for my left side, but all I received was a slight nick. I'm sure that you too have had an experience like this or know someone who has. The power of Qi is truly amazing.

Another particularly effective use of this practice is to help heal the sick. When you are bouncing, you can bring up the sickness of the patient and then put it out beyond the boundaries. The different organ networks are represented by the Five Element Animals. If any of these come up when you are bouncing, or if you already know what condition your patient has, put the animals beyond the circle until they fade away and disappear. The heart is represented by the Monkey, the spleen by the Ox, the stomach by the Pig, the lung by the Tiger, and the liver by the Dragon and the Horse. This will be a great aid to any other treatment the patients are receiving.

Some things you won't be able to shake off so easily. For these, you need to capture and burn them with sacred fire. Before you can burn them, you must first halt them in their tracks with a special incantation: "Rang Yang Kang." Repeat these words over and over out loud in an undertone, as if reciting a mantra, until the spirit is rooted to its spot. If you are familiar with the movie *The Legend of White Snake*, you will remember the scene where the master is trying to capture the snake spirit woman. In order to prevent her from moving, he calls out these words and she freezes, unable to move. The words' meaning is obscure, but when you pronounce them, you want to run them all together under your breath, until they flow together in a stream of sound. This talisman acts as a kind of sound vibration of control.

These words can also be used in dealing with disease. If there is a tumor or some other kind of growth, saying these words will stop the condition from spreading or even make it contract. Dr. Wu has used this technique with good results in his medical practice. He suggests that you try it the next time you're not feeling well. Say "Rang Yang Kang" over and over until you have the feeling of the illness under control. Then, concentrate your sickness into a small spot and go to the bathroom, eliminating it out of your body. This book gives you the methods. It's up to you to try it in your daily life.

Once you've gotten the entities to stay where they are, you are going to seal them in a special talismanic container so they can't escape. You must seal the "front door" and "back door" of this space; even though you are locking them in, you must leave a slight opening so that you can get rid of them. If instead you want to catch a ghost and keep it, you have to lock it up tightly, with the front, back, top, and bottom all welded shut. But to eliminate the ghost, you provide it with a little room in the back to slip out. How do you seal the front door? Say the word Qian (pronounced *chien*) three times. This refers to the Heaven trigram, the three solid lines. Even if you don't say the word out loud, you must visualize the image of this trigram three times in your mind. After the front door has been sealed, you're going to close the back door, leaving a space for the ghost to leave. Three times, say the word and visualize the image of Kun, the three broken lines of the Earth trigram. Feel both of these trigrams in your heart as you invoke them (fig. 46).

FIGURE. 46

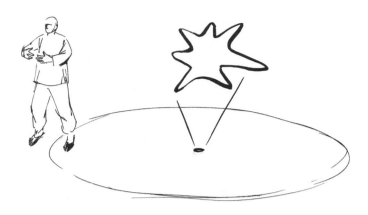

Remember that through all of this you have been standing on the rim of your circle. Yu Wei, the name of that inconspicuous place off to the side, is a very important principle to remember at this point. When sealing your ghost, you must stand in a place that is Yu Wei. Stand off to its side, perpendicular to it. Don't face the ghost directly or have your back to it. Use the sides of your body, just as in martial arts. If you come at someone at an angle to the body rather than head on, it will be easier to push the person off balance while using less of your own strength. This doesn't mean when you are practicing this Qi Gong, that you move your feet anywhere. Just hold these images in your mind (fig. 47).

Once you've captured your ghost, you must open yourself up to the great flowing power of the universe. Feel as if you are turning into a large mighty river, a vast lake, a high mountain, until finally you become the great ocean. Fill yourself with its power. Remember the canyons carved into the earth by the unrelenting force of water. Hold this meditation until you feel this body and soul. You need to be taken over by it. It's a physical sensation. By doing this, you have made yourself and your energy field completely fluid. In this state, you are ready for the final operation (fig. 48).

Nine wells must be dug. This is why we say, if you don't understand Qi Gong, how can you do Feng Shui? You need to use the Qi from your breath to dig these wells. If you don't put air into a beach ball, it's just a flat piece of rubber. When you blow it up, it becomes a ball and you can bounce it around. Airplanes need currents of air, or Qi, or stay up in the sky. You have already created a streaming liquid force all around you. Now use your Qi to dig the wells (fig. 49).

FIGURE. 48

Inhale through the nose, then "swallow" it down as far as it will go. There is no more lower Dan Tian, or lower abdomen, or even ground beneath your feet. Throughout this entire process, but no more so than now, your consciousness is operating in an abstract space with no relation to normal material properties like time and three-dimensional space. This takes sustained concentration and a lot of imagination; let the flow of the Qi help you, and you will be able to

HA!

FIGURE. 49

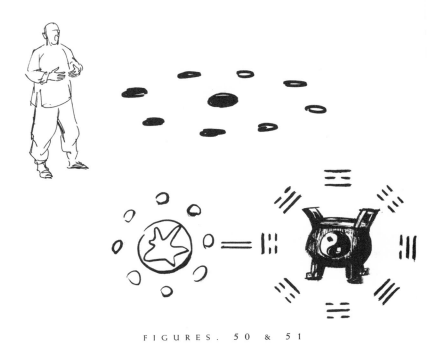

FIGURES. 50 & 51

fall right into it. If you trust the currents of Qi to support you, it will be easy to stay afloat and navigate quite nicely, too. It's actually a very liberating experience, if you choose to have it. Just let your hair down, loosen your tie, and go.

Inhale, send the Qi down as far as you can, and then let it rebound back up and out of your mouth in an exhale—"ha." By the time the Qi from your mouth reaches the ground, the well will be dug. The only difference between this "ha" and the one used earlier in the breathing pattern to bring out the light, is that in the previous case the Qi is not swallowed all the way down but is circulated from your head to your chest before it is exhaled. This leads to a shorter, more plosive exhale. When digging the wells, the Qi is travels a longer distance, and there's more of it, so even though the shape of your mouth is basically the same, your "ha" is going to come out sounding a bit softer, more breathy. The Qi should come up your throat and out of your mouth in a different way.

When Dr. Wu teaches this exercise, he doesn't go into lengthy explanations such as these; but then again, he's right there demonstrating, guiding, and helping the Qi along. In lieu of learning from a master, a thoughtful explanation of the proper breathing techniques is essential. Breath is Qi is the Tao. Understanding the dynamics of Qi and how to use the body as an instrument for directing it, is the mark of a true Qi Gong practitioner. It's really not that hard. Just relax your body and allow yourself a little playfulness. How a bird flies in the air or a dolphin swims in the water is how all of us have the capability of effortlessly and creatively interacting with the Qi. Without this realization, none of the information in this book would hold any meaning.

Make eight wells with your breath surrounding your ghost, and then drop a final well right in the middle to bury and seal the ghost for good (fig. 50). Let the nine wells blend together and become a Bagua Lu— an eight-trigram Taoist furnace (fig. 51). *Lu* literally means "stove" or "furnace." When the Monkey King was creating havoc in heaven, Lao Tze burned him in his alchemical cook pot in just this way.

Once the ghost is sealed inside your furnace, you are ready to burn it. Bring up the fire and heat from inside of you. What is this fire? It is known as Wu Ming Huo—the nameless, ineffable fire. There are no thoughts in your mind, only peace. There is no striving to be good, to be successful, or to be in a higher position. To begin the burning

FIGURE. 52

Jin Gan Bu Huai Gong

1. Relax; empty the body.
2. Open the Fa Gates. Inhale through the nose, swallow to the lower Dan Tian, exhale through the mouth and out the arms, legs, fingers, and toes. Repeat until you are relaxed.
3. Switch on the body's internal radar system. Circle from the perineum to the navel to the Ming Men, to the navel, thirty-six or seventy-two times. Circle horizontally from navel to Ming Men to navel between twelve and thirty-six times.
4. Bring out the light. Three inhales through the nose, one exhale ("ha") through the mouth. Repeat nine sets until the body feels hot.
5. Create the circle. Stand in the Yu Wei position. Open the space by stepping back two, three, or five steps.
6. Bring out the Ling Qi. Bounce and vibrate your circle outward, hands and arms rounded, until you have reached the edge of the universe.
7. Place Ling Qi three measures outside of the circle. Test to make sure it stays outside and disappears.

process, you must not have these thoughts in your mind. You must be completely at peace. Radiate this righteous fire from your heart. Heat your furnace until the evil beings and sickness melt away (fig. 52).

Don't disbelieve this practice. It may sound childishly simple, but it works. If you are able to accomplish these four stages of powerful mind work, you can turn back the clouds from the sky. You can bring rain and repel earthquakes. You can cure the sick. You can obtain the

8. Fix the Ling Qi in place with the "Rang Yang Kang" incantation.

9. Lock the front and back doors. Use the Qian and Kun trigrams. Say their names and visualize their forms, three times each.

10. Open yourself to the cosmic force of water. Hold it until your body flows.

11. Dig the nine wells. Inhale through the nose, swallow down as far as you can, exhale through the mouth— "ha." When the Qi lands, one well has been dug. Form eight wells around Ling Qi and put the ninth well in the center.

12. Transform the nine wells into an eight-trigram Taoist furnace, with the Ling Qi sealed inside.

13. Burn the Ling with Wu Ming Huo, the nameless Fire, keeping your mind clear and peaceful. Alternately, pray for the harmless Ling until it is at peace.

14. Draw the Faith Talisman. With your left hand, trace a line from left to right at the navel. Then, for men, draw a central line curving to the right. For women, curve the line to the left.

longevity of the ancients. The Immortal, Peng Tzi, is said to have lived to be eight hundred years old by doing this practice. It may seem simple, but it's very important.

At times, you may not want to burn the spirits you have caught. If they are not harming anyone, there is no need to destroy them. Pray for them instead. Once, Dr. Wu did this practice for a couple whose young girl was crying all the time. Outside, at the edge of their swimming pool, he started to vibrate and bounce out an energy form. After a few more shakes, its true form came through. It was a couple, a man and a woman. The paired spirit was the soul of a two-thousand-year-old rock near the pool. The presence of water had brought out its Ling. When Dr. Wu communicated with the spirit, it refused to leave. The stone had been resting in that particular spot for a long time and had grown quite comfortable there. It was also helping the father of the house in his career. Dr. Wu was faced with a dilemma. The spirit was good for the head of the household but bad for the women of the family, especially the daughter. In the end, he decided not to burn it, but the family had to put a fence around the pool and apply Xiong Huang wine, a specially prepared infusion designed to keep negative forces at bay. Preventing the bad but keeping the good is the Taoist way.

At times, when Dr. Wu treats his patients, he does this same prayer ritual. The day before he treats his patients, he prays for them. In the morning, he concentrates on the images of all his patients getting well as his first thought when he awakes. Dr. Wu feels this type of prayer can be more effective than psychological therapy. Both certainly work well together. As noted in the preceding chapter, the power of the mind to do good is remarkably strong. Talking to your plants, telling them to grow, will result in healthier plants. From the big perspective, if five hundred million people get together and think one thing, their combined thought could change the world. The lamas of Tibet practice this Nien Li—or prayer power—for the human race. Whether you practice the Heart Secret, Mystic Practice, Nien Li, or your own invented type of prayers doesn't really matter. Whether you are a doctor, a therapist, or a Feng Shui master, your skills won't help unless you wish other people well.

Finish the ritual by drawing a talisman of peace and protection on your body (fig. 53).

FIGURE. 53   The dot is located at your middle Dan. The semicircle is on the solar plexus. You do not need to trace these two points with your hand, but you must visualize them on your body. The lower figure is traced using the first and middle fingers of the left hand, with the rest of the fingers and palm gently cupped (fig. 54). Both men

FIGURE. 54

and women begin on the left side, moving up and across over the navel. Then, at the navel point, the fingers trace straight down about 2-½ inches. For men, this line then curves around to the right and the hand comes down to the side. For women, the curve goes back to the left and then down. As you can see, you have formed the Sanskrit symbol of AUM with your body (fig.55). The Taoists call this the Faith Talisman. This is the completion of the ritual.

This form of Qi Gong holds many profound mysteries. It is the prerequisite for stepping into the world of Taoist Feng Shui. Privately held within the Zheng Yi teachings for nearly 1,700 years, it is among the pinnacles of Taoist achievement and is the foundation for all of Taoism's most esoteric practices. It must be approached with respect and deep sincerity. The beauty of a large tree, with all its majestically spreading branches, still lies in its roots. Without them, the tree could not live. To learn and understand Feng Shui, you must encounter the mental and physical experience of the Jin Gan Bu Huai Gong. It is the engine that drives your ability to alter your life. Remember, your life's destiny is predetermined, but how you live it is where your opportunities lie.

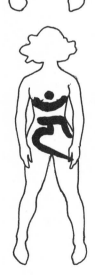

FIGURE. 55

6

Animal-Vegetable-
Mineral

As you can no doubt see by now, there is a direct relationship between the energy of living things and Feng Shui. After the land or home has been purified, there may be still more adjustments to make in order to counterbalance architectural or environmental conditions. In studying the *I Ching*, we are searching to create balance. To achieve harmony in nature, we must use the principles of the natural world and the energies of its inhabitants. Remember, everything living has Qi. Like goes with like. Counteract a negative with the thing that naturally controls it. Opposite energies in the right proportions can neutralize evil and give birth to positive new energy. All things—animal, vegetable, or mineral—have Qi that can help us.

Animal Forces

BIRDS AND FISH

Birds play an integral role in the world of Qi. Taoists believe that birds developed from fish. Water and fish represent wealth, so having fish or birds as pets can be beneficial. In the Tao, birds are considered more important than fish, but they serve an equally important purpose in the home. There are two things that must be kept in mind when having birds or fish as pets. Most importantly, you have to make sure their color matches the color of your birth season. This is imperative. A person born in the spring should have a green fish, someone born in the autumn may only have a white bird, and so on. There is one exception. Fish in your office must correspond to the birth color of your wife. Business will boom. This is a secret of Taoist Feng Shui that is known to very few. If you are a woman who owns her own business, the fish should match your own birth color. A single man without a girlfriend or wife uses his own color, too.

Dr. Wu went to the ranch of a well-known actor to teach him Qi Gong. He noticed a large aquarium filled with black fish. Dr. Wu told the client that the fish were the opposite color of his summer birth time. Not only should he replace them with red ones, he would be better off altogether having birds instead, due to his profession. You must take your career into account. If you are an architect or designer, birds are better than fish; but if you own a restaurant, then fish would be better. Use your imagination to find the correspondence of your work to the sea and the sky.

If you have a fish tank, make sure it has a pump that keeps the water circulating. You only want fresh, flowing water inside your house, to represent money flowing in. The tank should not be too tall or placed too high off the ground. It could subconsciously influence you to feel like you are drowning. Pictures of friends and family, especially of those who have passed away, should not be hung above a fish tank. Also, never face your fish tank toward the kitchen. The kitchen represents fire. It will burn the good influence of the fish and bring down their benefit.

Even if you can't keep a bird as a pet, having feathers hung up around your doorposts can repel evil influences. The White Cloud Monastery has feathers hung in all four directions around its doors. If you find feathers near your house or business, take them and hang them up. Don't look far away from home for your feathers. If they are lying on the ground outside of your house, consider them a gift from the universe. Also, it's good if friends give you feathers, but you can't ask for them in advance. This is a strict rule about feathers. In the monastery, when Dr. Wu was little, the whole front door of his living quarters was covered in feathers given to him as gifts. If the wind blows your feathers away, it's not a bad thing; but never throw them away yourself.

ROOSTERS

Along with the energy of live animals in your house, symbolic representations of their power are used for many different circumstances. The rooster has a special place in the bird kingdom that gives it especially helpful properties for Feng Shui. When the cock crows at dawn, the daylight comes. All the negative Yin forces, ghosts, and evil spirits are chased away. At the rooster's call, Yang begins to arise. It's an announcement for the dark forces to go home. If you put a rooster in your house and position it correctly, their troublemaking can be kept at bay.

There is a symbol of bad luck known in Chinese as Wu Gong Jen (fig. 56). It's shape can curse your house. Streetlights and electrical poles with wires stretching out have this sort of shape. Dr. Wu has many times treated entire families suffering from arthritis and other joint problems by putting a porcelain rooster inside their home. The Qi

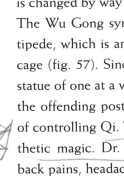

is changed by way of the principle of correspondences. The Wu Gong symbol resembles a caterpillar or centipede, which is an analog of the human spine and rib cage (fig. 57). Since roosters eat centipedes, placing a statue of one at a window, with its beak pointing out at the offending posts and wires, will stimulate a current of controlling Qi. This is the epitome of Taoist sympathetic magic. Dr. Wu has had many patients whose back pains, headaches, and arthritis have been alleviated by the power of this Feng Shui placement.

FIGURE. 56

Roosters are also good for houses with beamed ceilings or with pillars and posts. These beams and posts give a house the look of being segmented into many pieces, which subconsciously can lead to body pain. Use a porcelain rooster to take care of the problem. Just make sure it is a rooster with a comb (not a hen) and that the mouth is directly facing the trouble spot, not the side or tail. Only one rooster works. Too many roosters will cause a cockfight. Also, if you were born in the Year of the Rabbit, you cannot put a rooster in your house because these two signs are in conflict. Instead, use mirrors or crystals to reflect the unwanted energy back on itself. More information on this procedure will be given later in this chapter.

DRAGONS

In Taoist Feng Shui, the art of seeing and making imaginative connections is as important as developing the body's ability to harmonize with nature. The two are perfectly interrelated. Using animal symbolism in

Feng Shui is a thought-provoking way to discover this connection for yourself and your family.

The dragon lives in the waters of the earth and sky. It has the power to turn over the clouds and send down the rain. Water equals wealth. The dragon will bring you money. If business is not going well at the office, or if your household finances are beginning to feel squeezed, it's time to put in a dragon. Especially if your business is involved with the stock exchange, real estate, or banking, you should have a dragon.

Your dragon can be a statue or a picture. If it is a statue or figurine, it should be made of materials that look glossy, slippery, or translucent and thereby remind you of water. If it is a painting, it must be mounted in a gold frame. Do not use wood. Wood will block the dragon. Metal is best and, of course, gold-toned metal is perfect. The three best colors for a dragon, in order of desirability, are deep, almost black, blue-green (the ancient Chinese color, qing), red, and yellow.

Any portrayal must contain exactly one, two, four, or nine dragons. Three dragons are bad. Any other number will not be effective. Traditionally, when a dragon or rooster is drawn, a special day and time is picked to draw its eyes. The entire painting is completed first. The eyes are the final, most important touch. There are very specific standards involved. The eyes must not be narrow or too wide. The pupil of the eye is painted last of all. The way to tell whether a dragon painting has been properly done is to look at its eyes. The dragon's eyes should seem to focus on you and follow you around the room. Every time you look at it, from any vantage point, its gaze should be fixed upon you.

The dragon being a symbol of water, it's very important to know how to position it properly. When Dr. Wu visited a friend whose wife had just lost her job, the first thing he noticed was a dragon painting hung beside the fireplace. The dragon was being burned by the fire. He told his friend to move it next to the kitchen sink. The very next day,

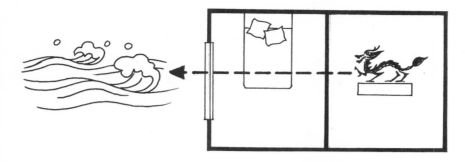

his wife was hired at a new job. The dragon supports the water element; it must be placed facing water—the ocean, a river, a stream, a fountain, or even a faucet. If you put a dragon by a sink, though, you must make sure it isn't in the bathroom or the laundry room. The dragon needs clean, incoming water, not dirty water being flushed out, as in the bathroom. Your money will be flushed away.

Making sure the dragon does not come near a bathroom is so important that if in placing your dragon facing a body of water, its gaze must pass through an adjoining bathroom first, it will cease to be effective altogether. Another room dragons should not be in or face toward is a bedroom, even if the room looks right out onto the ocean (fig. 58). Don't place a dragon in a hallway between two bedrooms, either. You can position a dragon facing north, which is the direction of water. This is helpful when you are not located near a body of water or when there is no sink with incoming water. (Faucets in an office always indicate outgoing water and should be avoided.)

Never put down carpets or rugs with a design of dragons woven in. It is the nature of dragons to fly up and go to the sea. If you step on them, they won't be able to take wing, and their powers will be defeated. A Chinese folk method of revenge is to write down your enemy's birth time and date on strips of paper and keep them in your shoes. As you walk around on them all day, they will be under your feet. Your enemy will be controlled and kept down, unable to do you harm. Dr. Wu does not advocate revenge, but he has seen this method work. So, let your dragons, the bringers of the waters of fortune, fly free.

QILIN

The dragon is the lord of the sky. Its counterpart on land is the marvelous *qilin*, sometimes translated into English as "unicorn." The qilin has only a minimal resemblance to this Western model. It is said to be an emblem of perfect harmony, as an incarnation of the Five Elements. Take a look at a bottle of Kirin beer. Kirin is the Japanese name for qilin and the picture on the bottle label is a representation of this mythical beast. It is an omen of good fortune and prosperity and is said to live for a thousand years. A pair of qilin, male and female, can be kept inside the house or, preferably, outside to bring peace and protection.

TURTLES

Another symbol of longevity is the tortoise. In Taoism, all big turtles represent long life. Many representations of turtles have been unearthed in the ancient tombs of China. Having a turtle in the house brings longevity and gets rid of sickness. It should be placed in the direction that corresponds to the material it is made of. For a wooden turtle, place its head facing east or southeast. A stone turtle should face southwest. Place a clay, ceramic, or porcelain turtle facing north, and a brass or iron turtle facing west.

Turtle shells get rid of ghostly presences and evil. Hanging your pots and pans from a ceiling rack in the kitchen works on the same principle; a wok has the same round form as a turtle's back. Too many pillars or sharp jutting corners in a house can be harmful. The curve of a turtle shell, hung opposite of these uncomfortable angles, will have a mitigating effect (fig. 59). Finding turtle shells can be a little tricky. Live turtles

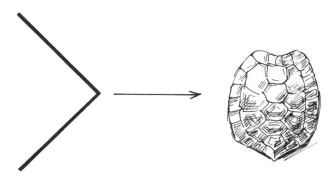

FIGURE. 59

or soup in Chinese fish markets or restaurants, and
illing to let you have the leftover shells if you ask.

HORSES

Having a horse in your office can, at times, be very fortuitous. Horses
represent success. They gallop as fast as the wind, speeding you to your
destination. They seem to be in flight, their hooves hardly touching
the ground. Especially if you work in transportation, such as selling cars
or driving a taxi, a horse is for you. When Dr. Wu was approached by
a consortium of Chinese airline company officials looking for advice on
doing business in the West, he recommended that the airline use a
horse as its figurehead.

If you choose to use a horse in your office, you must place it
where you want it at a particular time of the day. Invite the horse into
its new home between 11 A.M. and 1 P.M., the hours of the day when
the Yang Qi is at its height. You may use one horse or eight horses. For
a large waiting room, grand lobby, or corporate headquarters, a group-
ing of eight horses is best. For general office work, you don't need to
use eight horses. One will be fine. Never use five horses. Five horses are
the symbol of being drawn and quartered, a terrible punishment
reserved in ancient times for the most heinous capital offenses. Five
horses will tear you apart. You need not face your horse in any particular direction, but if you want to be a stickler, south would be fine.

DOGS

The dog is your guardian. In temples throughout China, one sees the famous Fu dog statues ("heavenly dogs" in Chinese). Dogs also bring in money. If you own a business and are looking for a receptionist, you should hire a person born in the Year of the Dog, no matter how young or old the person may be. Dog people are cheerful and hardworking. As long as your own animal sign is not incompatible with dog people, they will bring you fortune.

Wealthy countries always have many dogs. Dr. Wu once sent a letter to the city council of Beijing suggesting a campaign to encourage dog ownership in the city. Lots of dogs would bring lots of money, he argued. The mayor thought his proposal was ridiculous and threw the letter away. In fact, until recently, the city policy was to discourage pets, especially dogs, as an unnecessary waste. As a Taoist, though, Dr. Wu knew that more dogs would be a good thing. Nowadays in Beijing, having a dog has become a trendy fashion and people's fortunes are on the rise. Which came first, the chicken or the egg? A Taoist would say it was the dogs.

Whether you have a live dog or a Fu dog, it should be at the back of the house. Money might slip through the back door, so a dog should be at guard there. Dogs not only bring you money; they protect it, too. You can let your dogs run around in the front yard, but the doghouse should always be out back. Be careful when you purchase a Fu dog statue. They can look quite similar to traditional statues of lions, which have very different properties. Make sure you know exactly what you are getting. If you were born in the Year of the Dragon, you shouldn't have a dog in the house at all.

As for cats, a little story will serve to illustrate the Taoist opinion. Bao Gong, the great judge of the Song Dynasty, was once faced with a particularly difficult case. Interviewing the various parties, there was no way even such a wise counselor as he could discern who was lying and who was telling the truth. As a last effort, he invoked his occult powers and summoned a cat from the Yin Hells to decide the judgment. The cat, being highly skilled at smelling fish and catching rats, went straight for the true offender, who was taken away and punished. Bao Gong was so impressed with the acuity of the hell cat, that he decided he would keep it. He refused to let the cat go back home. This is why to this day, when you hear a cat cry, it's really the demon cat complaining that it wants to go back to hell. For a Taoist, dogs are positive Yang, and cats are negative Yin. Other mystical traditions, including the Jewish Kabbalah, also mention the dangers of keeping cats and their strong ties to the realm of the dead. Strictly speaking, cats are not recommended as pets.

LIONS

One cat that can overpower evil is the biggest cat of them all, the lion. Among the animal remedies, a pair of lions, male and female, can have the most dramatic effect on a place's Feng Shui. But lions must be used with extreme care.

Generally speaking, lions can be placed at the front door and nowhere else. One person told Dr. Wu she had bought a lion statue and liked it so much, she put it on her roof. He told her to take it down. Lions don't fly. They belong on the ground where they are king. When Dr. Wu was reading Feng Shui in Las Vegas, he pointed out that the lion's head at the entranceway to the MGM Grand Casino was not a good sign at all. Sitting, as it was, without a body, it suggested a negative omen. The severed head of a lion is a symbol of submitting to one's death. The owners of the casino were none too pleased to hear this, but the lion's head has since been taken down. A lion's head door knocker on your front door is an exception. It's reminiscent of the Chinese battle shields engraved with the image of a tiger that would be hung on the door to protect against evil spirits. Heraldic crests can also be used on the front door to serve the same purpose.

Lion statues are another matter. The owners of a furniture shop that had once been doing well called Dr. Wu asking for a Feng Shui reading. He warned them it would be expensive, but they insisted he come. Business was down, they said, now that a new Target department store had just opened across the street. Dr. Wu drove over to the furniture shop and circled around for twenty minutes, until he was convinced he was going to have to pull out the big guns. He told the owners he should have asked for ten times what he had originally asked for, because in order to help them, he would have to do something that would do harm to others. The good thing was that their business would shoot straight up; the bad thing was the Target store would have to close down.

The owners were very skeptical. There was no way a brand-new Target outlet was going to go out of business, they thought. Dr. Wu told them to keep their money. If the store across the street closed down within three months' time, they could pay him then.

One and a half months later, the Target store shut its doors. The shop owners came across town and personally delivered the money to Dr. Wu. Dr. Wu had placed a pair of stone lions outside their shop. Lions are very effective. In all his years as a Feng Shui master, Dr. Wu has helped place seventeen pairs of lions with a zero failure rate. If they are placed at just the right angle and with just the right timing, lions can create significant change. The drawback is that those they face will be harmed.

For example, there was another furniture store with two big stone lions out front. No matter what kind of business occupied the store directly across the street, it would always fail. The current tenants of this store were struggling with the lions. The husband kept on losing jobs and the kids were doing poorly in school. They approached Dr. Wu and accused him of putting up the lions. He assured them he had nothing to do with it and said he would come over at eleven o'clock in the evening and take a look.

Whoever had put those lions in place certainly knew their business because they were in the perfect position. The lions were controlling all of the other businesses on the block, pushing them down. Dr. Wu told the shopkeepers to spend some money to hire workers to turn the furniture store's lions out of alignment just enough so it wouldn't show. Then, they would have to chip a small piece of stone from each lion's hind quarters. Finally, at their own house, they would have to put two qilin on the roof. After two months, the owners of the furniture store moved out of that location. The spell had been broken and turned back around upon them.

Lions are so powerful, you even need to be careful if you take a snapshot of yourself standing next to one at the zoo. At the bottom of the photo, you must write, "This lion is accompanying me." Be sure not to stand right in front of the lion's mouth or it will eat you alive. Stand to the side and then take your pictures.

In general, don't put lions in front of your house. Doing so will be harmful. As mentioned earlier in the chapter, for houses, use qilin. In either case, they must be a pair, a male and a female. One very wealthy man that Dr. Wu had met through a friend had, without knowing, put a pair of what turned out to be male lions in front of his house. He admitted to Dr. Wu that from the time the lions had gone up, his life had taken a turn for the worse and he had lost a lot of money. He just hadn't known enough to have made the connection any earlier. Lions always do some damage to others. This is why, in all his years of practicing Feng Shui, Dr. Wu has only used lions seventeen times. He took a lesson from the experience of his teacher, who in 1949 had placed two stone lions in front of the South China Government Center facing out at the South China Sea; this was the decisive factor that helped force Chiang Kai Shek back to Taiwan. From then on, Dr. Wu decided he could only use lions in the most serious circumstances.

Once, while still living in Japan, Dr. Wu was approached by a distraught woman with a shocking story. Both she and her husband, professionals with Ph.D.s from Mainland China, had come to Tokyo to get their second doctorates. They moved in with her aunt, whose husband had died and left her a restaurant. Before long, the troubled woman's husband, who had often cheated on her in the past, started having an affair with her aunt. Then, the aunt forced her own niece into an underground prostitution ring and told her niece's husband that since his wife was sleeping with everybody in town, he might as well divorce her so the two of them could get married. The woman begged Dr. Wu for his help.

Dr. Wu checked around to see if her story was actually true. She was telling the truth. All she wanted now was punishment for the two people who destroyed her life. Dr. Wu told her she must promise that she would leave her life as a prostitute behind and start over, earning her money honestly. He would watch her for three years to make sure she wouldn't slip back into sex work. After three years, she returned to Dr. Wu. She told him her life was going well, but she still was determined to see her ex-husband and aunt pay for what they had done to her.

Dr. Wu tried to reason with her. He told her that since she was a Buddhist, she should know that "as you put down the knife you achieve enlightenment." All her sufferings would become blessings, opening a clear view of heaven before her eyes, if she could only let go of her craving for revenge. She insisted that that was impossible. In her mind, she had been reduced to the level of wanting revenge precisely because of what her aunt and husband had subjected her to. Dr. Wu felt that since she put it that way, he was going to have to help her.

He told the woman to bring him two small wooden lions. They had to be red. He told her to bury them fifteen feet away from the house where her aunt and ex-husband now lived, and to bury them in a particular direction. After forty-nine days, she would have to return to Dr. Wu and tell him what happened. After the forty-nine days had passed, the woman returned to Dr. Wu with a newspaper clipping. The aunt and the husband had died together in a car crash on a busy highway. Dr. Wu believed they deserved their fate for the abuse that had dehumanized this tragic woman. Use of lions for Feng Shui must be taken very seriously. There are many lions around, but without the proper timing and placement, they do absolutely nothing. With the correct method, they work immediately. Dr. Wu recommends very strongly that if you are considering using lions, you pay for the services of a top Feng Shui master to position them for you. Feng Shui is a practice with many rewards, but its power must be respected.

Plant Life

As we have learned, you can never judge the Feng Shui just by the health of a garden. Plants may be growing well because there are dead animals decomposing in the ground. There may be energies attached to the land that are only visible to one who knows how to look. Nevertheless, trees and plants can have a very beautiful and healing Qi. There are many Qi Gong techniques that help one to commune with the vegetable kingdom. Just as there are many herbs and roots that give life to humans, each one for a different condition, living trees can provide a wide array of positive energies that can be used for health and welfare. In both the solar and lunar forms of Qi Gong, trees are used to help ground oneself, acting as one's first helpers when learning to exchange energy with other forms of life.

I'll always remember the first time I practiced an entire Qi Gong form on my own, without Dr. Wu's supervision. I was required to do the practice standing in front of a tree. I went to my local park and walked around and around, looking at all the trees until I found one that seemed just right. After I had finished the form, I felt I needed to lean back on the tree for a moment of rest. I was amazed, because instead of hard, dry bark, I felt a strong wave of soft, gentle energy rising up to meet me, like a big, warm hug. The Qi Gong had slowed me down enough to appreciate the loving life force that lived in the heart of that tree.

Later on, when I asked Dr. Wu about it, he told me that trees have personalities just as diverse as people's. Some trees will naturally click with you, and you will have a special bond with them, like two friends. Others will have little in common with you or will not want to be disturbed. Old trees are filled with the wisdom of their many rings. Their Qi gives out spiritual nutrition, much like a wise elder who shares his knowledge. Ancient trees can get rid of bad Qi. Some very old trees can become the seat of a personality too far removed from human energy for them to be safely approached. Young trees, no taller that yourself, are great for increasing energy and are easier for practicing Qi sharing with. Sick trees can pass their suffering along. Using the Qi Gong practices in this book, you can begin to discover the rewards of exploring the secret world of plants.

SHARING WITH PLANTS

As described in Chapter 4, the Mind Secret is a great way to communicate with the Qi of plants. Practice with any plants or small trees that appeal to you. If a particular plant smells good to your nose, it's a good sign the plant is right for you. Start absorbing the plant's Qi into your

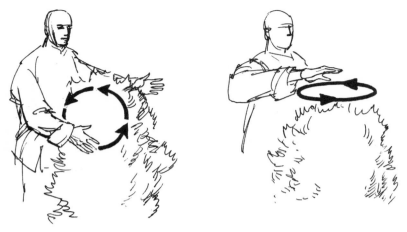

upper Dan. If you feel any discomfort or resistance, don't continue. The plant can't share with you right now. If it feels good, absorb the Qi for thirty to sixty seconds.

Here is another simple Qi Gong technique for putting plant energy into your body.

1. Early in the morning, stand in front of a small tree or shrub with your arms bent at the elbows, your hands on either side of the plant a few inches away from its surface, and your palms facing each other. If your hands feel comfortable, proceed to the next step. If they hurt or feel numb, try other plants until you find one more willing to share (fig. 60).

2. First with one hand and then with the other, circle your hand toward you, without touching the plant, until you feel the plant's Qi filling your hand and a connection forming between your heart and the plant. The hand that is not circling stays still (fig. 61).

3. When both hands feel full, place one hand above the plant, while the other hand stays in place. Move the hand on top of the plant in a flat circle until a strong sense of energy is felt,

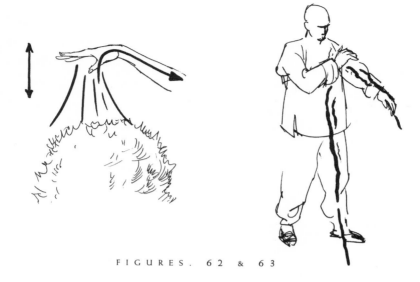

FIGURES. 62 & 63

then lift your hand gently up about a foot above the plant and bring it back down, as if you are pulling the Qi out of the plant through your palm and into your arms. Make as many passes over the plant as you need to in order to fill your arm completely with Qi. Again, the other hand remains still. When your arm feels full, repeat this step with the opposite hand (fig. 62).

4. Finish by rubbing the Qi that is in your arms up to the shoulders, down the front of the chest, over the hips, front and back, and then down the legs and out the toes and feet (fig. 63).

After you complete this practice, your body will feel very clean. You may continue at this point by practicing Qi Gong, T'ai Chi, or meditation. If you just can't seem to feel the energy of the plants at all, try swimming a few laps in a pool before trying again. These exercises will help you experience the relationship among humans, plants, and the environment.

Even though you cannot read the total Feng Shui of a house by

FIGURE. 64

the lushness of the plants, you can definitely alter its course by understanding the plants' contributions to the area. First, green symbolizes peace. Having plenty of green grass in the yard and green plants inside the house is very good for calming the environment. The color green relates to the eyes and the liver, which, in Chinese medicine, when cleansed, can be the source of peaceful emotions. Always having a lot of green things around to look at will stimulate the liver function and promote a sense of well-being.

If there are only one or two very large trees in your backyard, this can be a problem. The Chinese character for "difficulty" is *kuan* (fig. 64). The square represents the house and the figure in the middle means "wood" or "tree." Very large trees can bring difficulties. It's especially bad to have a tree like this right in the center of your yard. If you've ever observed very large trees, you will notice that their roots and the canopy of shade they form prevent other plants from growing around them. The psychological component of this can be transmitted to your family members and thereby bring them down. Also, the spirit of very old trees can affect the health of people living nearby. One large tree in the middle of the backyard can be too dominant. This situation can be easily adjusted by planting more vital, young trees in the yard. Make sure you have at least five trees in your backyard for balance. The best place for a very large tree is at the back of the yard, where it can add support and act as a "backbone" for your property.

Having a very large tree in front of your home, within fifty feet of it, can also be a problem. If you can't see the tree from inside the house, it's a little bit better, but if the tree directly faces your front door, something must be done to correct this problem. I have seen Dr. Wu treat this particular problem by hanging a small round mirror over the door frame to reflect the tree back at itself (fig. 65). Also, the sort of modern architecture that has trees growing partially inside of the house is a big no-no that should absolutely be avoided (fig. 66).

A dead or leafless old tree in front of the house is not good, either.

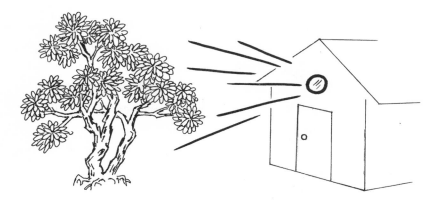

FIGURE. 65

This situation can be especially dangerous for elderly people. An old, dead tree can lead them to sickness or even death. Dr. Wu had a patient who suffered from severe eczema for over twenty years. The patient had been to see many Chinese doctors and American doctors, but none of them were able to bring him any relief. Even Dr. Wu was having trouble treating this patient, so he offered to come over and look at his house. As Dr. Wu walked around the yard absorbing the Qi, his body started to itch. The nearer he got to an old oak tree, the more violent the itching became. He told the man and his wife that the old tree was the source of the eczema problem. The advanced age and long history of this tree were affecting the man's health. The tree would need to be moved before it made the man any worse. They would have to take great care to ensure that the tree withstood the transplantation, for if it died, that could finish him off entirely. The wife got angry at Dr. Wu, accusing him of being a charlatan and of coming up with this harebrained idea to cover up his inability to treat her husband's condition.

FIGURE. 66

The man went ahead and looked into Dr. Wu's suggestion and found that, on top of everything else, moving the tree was going to be a huge production. It turned out that the tree was a California Live Oak, a protected species that would require a government permit to be moved. Also, the new location would have to be approved by an environmental panel, and the man would have to hire a special tree doctor to give the oak shots before and after transplanting to help ensure its survival. This whole procedure was not only going to be a bureaucratic nightmare, but it was also going to cost him $5,000. There was no way he was moving that tree.

Six months went by. The couple's finances had been doing well, but the man's condition had not gotten any better. He decided he might as well spend the money to move the tree. After all, he was at his wit's end. The tree was moved. One month later, after twenty years of misery, his condition had completely cleared up. This story may sound unbelievable, but it's true. Sometimes, when your body is sick, you have to move certain things around. You don't even have to believe in it for it to work.

Different types of trees have different qualities of energy and need to be placed in specific areas around the house to be beneficial. For example, Dr. Wu recommends Chinese red dates (jujubes) for his infertile patients. Medically speaking, red dates replenish the Qi. But red dates also work on a syncretic level because the Chinese word for them, zao, means "early." This allows for a pregnancy to arrive early. Bringing red dates to friends in the hospital is like saying, "Get well soon; get out of the hospital early." The developers of a new tract-home community were having trouble selling the units. Dr. Wu suggested that they plant red date trees in the backyards to bring things forward and make sales pick up. His suggestion worked; the houses started to sell. Another interesting tree whose properties involve wordplay is the apple tree. Pingguo means "apples," and ping an means "peacefulness." Bringing someone apples is to wish that person peace. Apple trees are also very good for planting in the front yard. Never bring pears to a sick person in the hospital—*Li* means "pear" and "to separate."

Besides apple trees, orange and persimmon trees are good in front of the house. Figs and poplars should only be planted in the backyard, where they work very well. Willow trees, especially in the front yard, are not a good idea. They have a lot of Yin Qi. Even in the West, they are thought of as "weeping willows." Bamboo represents hard work. It absolutely should never be planted in the backyard. It will break your finances down. You will work hard and still wind up broke. Bamboo on the sides of the house is also bad. It will make your money disappear. But bamboo is great in front of the house. Placed there, it brings in peacefulness. If you have bamboo growing around your house, dig it up and move it to the front.

There are guidelines for keeping plants inside the house as well. Since we are on the subject of bamboo, if someone gives you a gift of lucky Chinese bamboo, it should always be kept on a table, never on the floor. Bouquets of sunflowers, however, should be put on the floor, facing east toward the rising sun. Big plants with many broad, thick leaves help clean the environment in a room by releasing oxygen. Stay away from small plants and flowers. In this situation, bigger is better. Large plants are the best for collecting Qi. They will bring you money, especially if you put them in the best spot in the house. In your house's worst spot, put a cactus. The cactus is considered the king of plants. Put it in a dark corner with little airflow and it will adjust the environment. Its spines will also help repel negativity.

Live plants are always preferable to cut flowers. In hotels and houses, never put out huge bouquets or floral arrangements. As they die, cut flowers absorb a lot of oxygen, so you want to go easy on them. Never keep them in the bedroom. Dried flowers and silk, paper, or plastic plants are also not good. Again, they should be kept out of the bedroom. Artificial plants are acceptable for an office.

Remember, green brings peace. When Dr. Wu does Feng Shui at the house of a family that quarrels a lot, he first wants to know who fights more, the husband or the wife. It could be either. Men have bad tempers. Women might be going through menopause. Once the instigator is determined, he knows on which side of the house to put plenty of plants. He orients himself going out of the house as "south." For men, the plants are put on the left ("east") side of the house, and for women, on the right ("west"). This works very well. Green will cease the war.

The Mineral Kingdom

Rocks have a life force that plays as important a role in Feng Shui as do plants. It may not seem so on the surface, but rocks can be alive or dead just like plants, and they can, with great age, house spirits and forces within them just like trees do.

Another old tale of Liu Bowen tells of how he brought the Third Black Rock over the Lu Gou Bridge. The general, after building Beijing in the shape of the eight-armed Nezha, was still concerned about protecting it from the floods sent by an evil dragon. He had heard of three holy black rocks on Shang Fang Mountain that had achieved sainthood; the first for ten thousand years, the second for five thousand, and the third for a thousand. Their spiritual power was strong enough to subdue all dragons and tigers. Liu Bowen decided that if he could get all three rocks to come to Beijing, the city would be secure for all time. He hastened over the Lu Gou river ford, but the rocks knew he was coming. After making offerings to them and politely requesting their help, he knew they weren't going to budge. He then pulled the forces of a heavenly army from his sleeve and commanded the rocks to come. Only the Third Black Rock succumbed to his power and started rolling along down the mountain.

Meanwhile, the evil dragon king and his son were erecting a blockade in the shape of a scorpion city, back at the ford of the river.

First, they built the Lu Gou Qiao, which still stands today (it is known in the West as Marco Polo Bridge). This was the scorpion's tail. East of the bridge they built a city, which was the body of the scorpion, with the two wells outside its east gate being the eyes. A little further east, they erected two mounds—one in the north, one in the south—to act as the scorpion's pincers.

The next morning, when the general arrived on the west bank of the river, he had no choice but to send the rock over the bridge. They would skirt south of the city to avoid crossing over the scorpion's back. The Third Black Rock stopped short of the bridge, afraid to go on, but the heavenly troops forced it along. Just as they were turning south on the other side of the river, the scorpion's tail lashed out at the rock, and it ceased to move forever more. Beijing was thus protected from floods, but to this day, the waters of the Lu Gou river regularly rise up to cover its banks.

This story wonderfully summarizes the whole spectrum of Taoist Feng Shui philosophy—from conceptualizing the shape of the terrain, to using the four directions, to exerting influence over the components of nature. Just as water is focused on economic issues, mountains and rocks correspond to political matters. Stones act as collectors and controllers of Qi. As mentioned in Chapter 4, training your perceptions with the Mind Secret and other Qi Gong practices will help you determine a live stone by its pleasing shape and energetic feeling. You must make sure your rock is alive before you can use it for anything.

The controlling nature of a healthy stone can calm jangled nerves. These stones dispel Zao Qi, hot and dry energy, by cooling it. When Dr. Wu's teacher read the *I Ching* for Mao Ze Dong, he would have him first lay down on a large stone. If you find the right stone, it can be used to keep the harmony of your marriage. A woman who was married to a very wealthy businessman came to see Dr. Wu. She was this man's fourth wife and she wanted to make sure she would also be his last. She felt she had good reason to be concerned for her marriage: Her husband would spend a lot of time at the nightclub he owned in

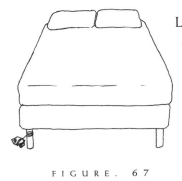

FIGURE. 67

Las Vegas. She introduced Dr. Wu to her husband; afterward, Dr. Wu took her aside and told her what to do. She needed to wrap a red thread around a small stone and tie it to the foot of their bed, opposite the side he slept on. Before, he would not always come home at night. After one month with the stone tied to the bed, he started coming home every night without fail. It's been over a year and their marriage is very peaceful.

This talisman, up until now, has been a Taoist secret. In Dr. Wu's experience, it has an 80 percent success rate for preventing infidelity. Preferably, the man should sleep on the left side of the bed and the woman on the right. The stone is wrapped in a red thread, which repels evil influences, and hung at the foot of the bed on the opposite side of the spouse under suspicion (fig. 67).

A dead rock can have a similar but much more dangerous effect. A young girl showed Dr. Wu the jade bracelet that her boyfriend bought for her. She was proud of it and wore it everyday. Dr. Wu took one look at it and said she might as well return it. It was made from a dead piece of jade. It is easy to see the life and energy in a piece of live jade, but the jade in this bracelet was dull and had cracks. He told her that wearing it would lock her up and leave her no way to escape. It would do her harm. When purchasing jewelry of any kind, you have to be extremely careful of what you buy. An expensive pendant could just as easily be dead as a cheaper one is alive. You have to know how to tell the difference.

Even healthy live rocks have to be used carefully. It's important to have some stones around when you practice Qi Gong, but you can't overdo it. If there are a lot of unexplainable occurrences taking place at your house, check out the rocks in the backyard. Having too many rocks at the back of the house is not good. If you sense something wrong or if you don't feel well, have the rocks moved away. You will

see good results very quickly. Avoid having large rocks or
front of your house entirely. Remember, everything must be in
for harmony to be achieved.

Dr. Wu visited a woman who had built a stone Zen garden ins.
of her house, just outside of the study. He was concerned that seeing
the heavy rocks every day would lead to a depressed, weighty feeling
of burden. Because the garden had it all—rocks, plants, water, and a
view with a sky full of clouds behind it—and because the woman's
career involved inspiration and creative thinking, a simple solution was
at hand. Dr. Wu told her to buy a bird and keep its cage on the stone
in the center of the garden. She would then have the Five Forests right
in her home. I visited this woman about a month after the Feng Shui
reading and I can attest to the fact that the mood in that corner of her
house had changed from slightly somber and flat to lively and refresh-
ing, almost like being outdoors in the country.

Crystals form a special category in the world of Feng Shui. A
crystal is a natural silicon formation extracted from the earth. It collects
Yin and radiates Yang. This special balance of energy gives crystals a
unique ability to harmonize the home or office. Crystals gather up the
universal messages from deep within the earth and focus the mind in a
manner that unites it with this information. To bring in inspiration and
cleansing light, a Taoist Feng Shui practitioner will most frequently use
a crystal.

The three types of crystals commonly used in Taoist Feng Shui
are round, diamond-shaped, and "purple mountain" or amethyst crystals. There are specific ways of using each type of crystal, which we will
discuss in this and the following chapters. A general tip is to make sure
the crystals are always brilliant and shining from within. If a crystal
looks cloudy or becomes dusty, wiping it with a cloth won't be enough.
There are a number of different ways to clean and reenergize a crystal.
Choose the one that works best for you. First, you can hold it under a
stream of water, either straight from the tap or poured overhead. Just
make sure the water isn't from a bathroom faucet. Then, let the crystal

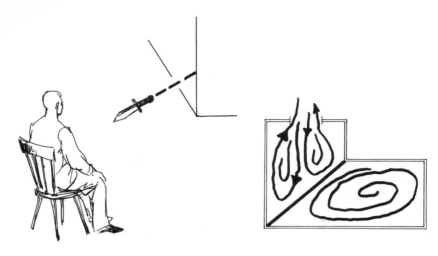

dry in the sun. Second, you can wash the crystal in the ocean or in another body of running water and let it dry in the sun. Finally, you can leave it in the freezer compartment of your refrigerator overnight. Whichever method you choose, you will notice the difference it makes in the crystal's appearance.

In Taoist Feng Shui, there is a concept called sharp peak intrusion. This is when the sharp point of an angle, such as from a building or road outside of your house or from a corner or pillar inside, focuses a harsh line of energy into your space. Examples include (1) two roads converging in a point that comes together directly opposite your house, (2) buildings whose corners abut your home, (3) square structural pillars inside the home, and (4) open or odd-shaped rooms with corners that break the square shape of the room. The energy that these harsh angles create is very invasive. Ideally, the flow of Qi should be freely unobstructed inside an open square, so you can see how having a sharp protrusion could be very disruptive (fig. 68). Just imagine yourself sitting in an easy chair that faces a concentrated beam of pointed Qi. It would feel like a knife in your heart. Even if the space directly opposite this edge is an empty area in your house, its line will break the natural flow of Qi in the room, either into a stagnant pocket (if there is no window or door) or to an area where the Qi just flows back on itself and out the opening it came in from (fig. 69). Any way you look at it, an unhealthy situation will exist.

Another line of energy that is very negative is the Ghost Line. It is created when your front door faces southwest or southeast. Even more important than the ideal location for your house is the direction in which your front door faces. As discussed in Chapter 2, ideally, you want to match its direction to your birth season. When this is not possible, you must always insist on a front door that points in a cardinal direction—south, east, north, or west. Facing north or northeast is bad enough, but facing southeast or, especially, southwest will stimulate the energy of the Ghost Line. All bad Qi from the universe originates in the southwest and southeast, including evil entities and some types of ghosts. The southeast is a major source of trouble. It will make your body go bad. The Qi from the southwest will make you lose money and meet with misfortune. Dr. Wu has kept track of this phenomenon. Every home he has ever visited whose occupants have had problems of stolen credit cards or being cheated out of money, has had the front door facing southeast on the Ghost Line.

How does one rectify these negative angles? Taoist Feng Shui practitioners may use crystals (alone or in special combinations), mirrors, wind chimes, lighting, animal shells, and written talismans. This may sound like quite a laundry list, but all these things share the ability to block bad Qi. The basic rule of thumb is this: To get rid of a negative line of Qi, either reflect it back on itself or deflect it by setting up a new line of Qi as a counterattack.

Mirrors reflect the Qi back on itself. They are good for indoor and outdoor use. A regular flat mirror reflects the Qi of a sharp angle or, in some cases, of a tree. For a particularly bad angle, use a concave mirror, which will suck the Qi in and more forcefully spit it back out. For use with a Ghost Line, or if you live facing a cemetery, hang a Bagua (eight-trigram) mirror (fig. 70). An eight-trigram mirror is specif-

ically designed for repelling evil spirits and ghosts and preventing them from reentering your home. Do not use this type of mirror to reflect a sharp angle. It is not made for this purpose, and it won't be effective. Mirrors used for reflecting purposes should always be hung high on the wall, pointing directly at the target angles (fig. 71). In cases involving a row of columns or ceiling beams, hang mirrors on either side of each line of the Qi all along the row (fig. 72). In most cases, the mirrors should be small and round. Round and spherical objects have a lot of vital, propulsive energy. Just like a wheel, they help things move forward (fig. 73).

Outside the home, in addition to mirrors, wind chimes can be hung. They must only be placed outdoors, where the wind can blow

FIGURES. 71, 72, & 73

through them; never put them inside the house. They should have only five chimes, for the tones that correspond to the Five Elements. Sometimes you can find wind chimes that have been specially tuned to the Chinese pentatonic scale, but pulling off a couple of rods to make five on a wind chime you already have is acceptable. Wind chimes disperse turbid Qi in the environment. They also break the Ghost Line. When they play their melody in the breeze, their sound warns all ghosts and demons to stay away. Inside the house, for sharp corners, you can hang a Chinese flute, the shao, to get rid of the angles (fig. 74). *Shao* means "to get rid of."
A turtle shell hung facing the angles will break them up with its curved shape.

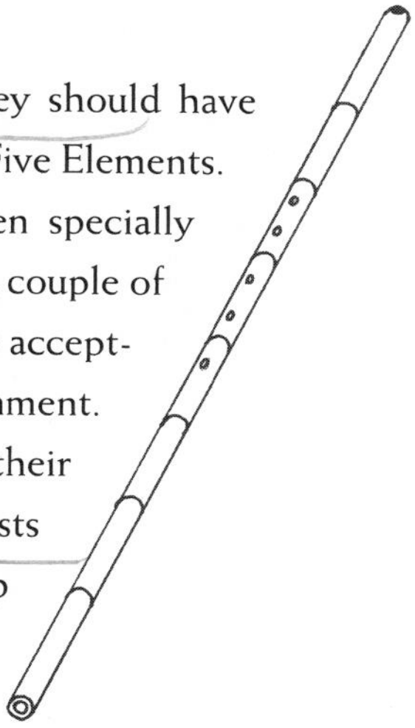

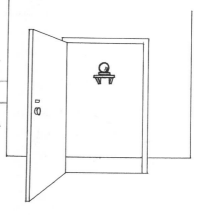

FIGURE. 74

Crystals do everything that mirrors do but with one major difference: Instead of simply reflecting the Qi back, crystals repel it with a stronger Qi of their own. This feature is especially important for outside facing roads or large buildings and for dingy, stagnant indoor areas that need illumination and revitalization. An example is a front door that opens directly on a wall. If it is a hallway, like with space, a small mirror wouldn't be enough. You would need either a wall full of mirrored paneling or a medium-sized crystal ball set in a wall sconce and suspended from the ceiling or placed on a small table, depending on the effect you want to achieve (fig. 75). In other words, mirrors are inspired by the moon (Yin), whereas crystals transmute their Yin energy into Yang. So, in a sense, crystals accomplish their purpose with a dynamic transformation, while mirrors function more like a traction beam, pulling things in and reflecting them back. Since Feng Shui is first and foremost a process of balancing Yin and Yang, only by judging the overall situation can you best

FIGURE. 75

decide what will work for you. As in a game of tug-of-war, sometimes you need to pull back with all your strength, and other times you need to lean in a little before pulling back to set the other side off balance.

Inside the house, one small to medium-sized clear crystal ball is usually set up on a table opposite the negative angle you want to neutralize. Frequently, a lamp is set up next to or behind the crystal ball, to add energy to its effect. At the very least, keep the light on when you are at home. Leaving it on around the clock is even more effective. Later in this chapter we will discuss a number of other key positions inside the house where crystal balls can be placed to illuminate your money-making potential and keep you safe at night.

Outside the house, crystals are buried in the ground, most commonly in one of two special patterns. They are put down to deflect negative Qi coming in at the front door, either a Ghost Line or an invasive angle. The two talismanic patterns can be formed using a wide range of other objects, from nails to small piles of rice, depending on the situation. You can even use glass marbles if you can't find or afford crystals. Remember, crystals represent change. If you use something that represents a crystal to represent change, you are still using the laws of sympathetic magic.

The first talisman is formed in the shape of a mountain (fig. 76). It is, always laid out with its peak pointing out at the angle you want to repel. It is buried in the ground five feet from your front door (fig. 77). The second talisman is positioned the same way (figs. 78 and 79). It is at times, stronger that the first talisman, but it is not always necessary. For example, if roads face your house at an angle, you use the mountain peak talisman, but you have to use three diamond-shaped crystals, not spherical ones. In this case, you could also use wood, metal, live rocks, or even nails, all placed in the same pattern. The corners of a house facing your front door is another example of when it's time to bury crystals, but in this case you can use either pattern and any type of crystals

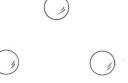

FIGURE. 76

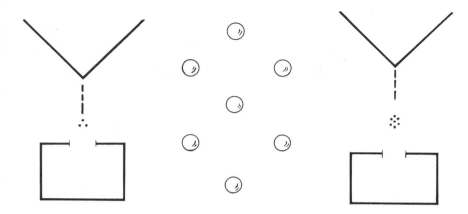

FIGURES. 77, 78, & 79

except purple mountain ones. You can also use turtle shells, or even oyster or clam shells. Either talisman can be used to rid yourself of a Ghost Line, but in this case use crystals, rocks, or turtle shells. If you have a problem with a Ghost Line or a hostile angle, by all means put down one of these talismans, even if you have to break up the sidewalk in front of your house to get it in the ground. You can prevent misfortune from coming to your home.

Inside the house, the seven formation can be put under the bed. This helps to collect Qi and wealth as well as to keep evil influences at bay, depending on what you use to arm the talisman. Piles of rice are for wealth and sustenance. Turtle shells keep away ghosts. Crystals are for all purposes, though diamond-shaped crystals are the most "sharply" energized. A concerned parent asked Dr. Wu what to do about his house. After he moved in, he found out someone had died in the house, which explained why he never felt safe and why his little boy cried all the time. Dr. Wu told him to place this talisman made of diamond-shaped crystals under both his son's bed and his own bed. Since then, the boy is doing fine and the house feels safe. The benefits of talismans cannot be explained scientifically. Again, you just have to believe.

In addition to reversing harsh angles, the energy of crystals can

FIGURE. 80

stimulate wealth and success. One very important place to keep a single clear crystal ball is in the far right-hand corner of your desk (fig. 80). Whether performed at home or in the office, this practice known as Shui Jing Gong (water crystal practice) is a powerful aid to concentration. It also can focus good fortune upon you as you work. Use a crystal ball that is in proportion to the size of your desk. This practice can also be done by placing any sort of white object in that corner of your desk. This is a strict formula. Don't keep a crystal ball anywhere else on your desk.

The second and most important technique for consolidating wealth also uses a crystal ball. When you open your front door at a

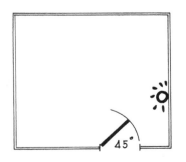

FIGURE. 81

forty-five degree angle, the first spot your eyes fall upon will be your prosperity position. Put a crystal ball and/or lamp right there, so that every time you come through the door, it will be the first thing you see (fig 81). If you don't have a crystal ball, keep a lit table or floor lamp there. You can even use a TV or computer monitor, just as long as the wealth position is illuminated. This location will help you accumulate wealth, money, and good Qi. By all means, try this placement in your home and office. It is among the most simple and fundamental Feng Shui ways to change your Qi.

Now that we have explored the methods of sensing Qi and of using the forces of the natural world to make adjustments, we will pull back our focus in the following chapter to observe the guidelines for positioning a home within the environment.

7

The Ideal
Environment

The sky above, the earth below, and all of us in the middle—this is the perfect vision of the Taoist universe. Knowing ourselves leads to understanding the world around us, and in turn, knowledge of the world leads to greater understanding of the self. At a very deep level, the Feng Shui of an environment has the power to support our search for self-realization and outward expression. Surrounded by harmony, we are aided in achieving balance for ourselves and for those whose lives we touch. When we look up at the clouds, or feel the soil between our fingers, we are ultimately examining our own souls.

In the *I Ching*, there is no easy way to resolve the number 5 and the number 7. Seeking wealth and achieving nobility of spirit are two very different paths that are difficult to reach together. The Taoists believe that certain very special locations can ensure the combination for you, your children, and your children's children. An older man came to Dr. Wu for help with finding a house on a spot like this. He wanted to give his children and grandchildren a gift that would bring them health, wealth, and all the riches life has to offer.

It took Dr. Wu some time to find the right property, and when he did, there was a family already living there. He knocked on the door, introduced himself, and started up a conversation. As it turned out, the present owners had not done that well themselves before moving into this house. Their restaurant business was steady but not exceptional and the children were having some problems. Now, the restaurant was doing fabulously and both children were attending Harvard. They insisted that Dr. Wu's client had to offer them $800,000, more than twice the market value of the house, before they would agree to sell it to him. Then, after the client purchased the house and moved in, his son's serious learning disability cleared up. Right away, he was able to count numbers and was starting to learn the alphabet. Even Dr. Wu could not find any sort of medical explanation for the boy's transformation. To find the dragon's body may sometimes be easy, but it is much harder to put light to its eyes.

The Lords of the Four Directions

The ideal location must contain mountains, trees, water, and gently curving pathways or roads. These elements correspond to the Four Directions. The east is ruled by the Green Dragon, the west by the White Tiger, the south by the Crimson Bird, and the north by the Black Turtle. In terms of a piece of property, standing at your front door looking out, you should be able to face south and see trees, and perhaps a small stream. To your left is the east, where a body of water, a pool, or even a faucet should be located. To the right is the west, home of the Tiger, symbolized by a road. Behind you in the north should be a mountain or small hill. If your home or office is located in the center, surrounded by these conditions, you have found the perfect place to replenish your Qi. If you have picked your location following the 3-6-72 rule, you may also look at the thirty-six buildings on either side of you, plus the streets in front and in back of you, to find possible correspondences to the elements belonging to the directions.

As an illustration of this principle, we will look at the location of Dr. Wu's medical clinic. The front door of his office opens to the south. The Tiger is to the right, and to the right of his office is the street. To

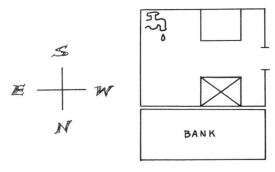

FIGURE. 82

the left is the men's bathroom, which has its faucet and water. This is how you would look at it. Upon opening his office door, you should be able to see the Bird, but there's just another office door opposite. This is not good. Behind the clinic is a bank that stands taller than its roof, which is only so-so. This isn't the perfect office location, but it's better than average. The main thing that is missing is the bird. There should have been an open field where there is only a door. Dr. Wu made sure to put bird feathers he had found around the clinic's door frame (fig. 82).

Next, we look at the orientation from the front door of the building (fig. 83). The actual direction looking out is west, but for this

FIGURE. 83

method of Feng Shui, we still consider it south. Again, to the left is the Dragon. Within thirty-six buildings to the left of his office building is a restaurant. This is okay; the Dragon is fine. To the right, not only is there a road but there is also that bank. Banks are involved with gold and metal. The Tiger is taken care of. Out in front of the office are trees and birds, a twenty-storey, black-glass building, and, six blocks down, the ocean.

One weakness of this location is that in front of the office is the ocean (the Bird is fire). Another is that the office is blocked by a tall building. But that building is made of glass, which is transparent. That makes it a little better; not perfect, but okay. If the building had been made of concrete or brick, it would have been much worse. If it hadn't been across the street with a road in between, it would have posed even more of a problem. Behind the clinic is an apartment house. People live there, creating human Qi. Mountain and Human thus correspond. If instead there had been an office building behind the clinic, the location would not have been as good; but if there had been a school full of children behind, it would have been a lot better. This then, is the way of Taoist Feng Shui.

Exercise

Look at the positioning, based on the view from the front door (or building entrance, if applicable), of your home or office. Stand looking out of the door "facing south" to check the following elements.

1. Water on your left (within thirty-six buildings to the left)
2. Road or metal-related things on your right (within thirty-six buildings to the right)
3. Birds, trees, fields, or fire-related things in front of you
4. Mountains or places with human Qi behind you.

In addition to fixing your home to correspond with the symbols of the Four Directions, it is very important to consider who will be living in the home and how the building fits in visually with the surrounding environment. Everything must go with the flow. Some of this is pure common sense. In *The Art of War*, Sun Tzu discusses environmental situations of placement. For example, if your troops were camped at the top of a mountain, you would have to consider what you would do if you were surrounded or if there was a fire. If you were down in the valley, you could be attacked from above, or you could be flooded out. Even today, it's typical for very low-lying areas to flood, or for brush and forest fires to erupt in mountainous areas. These are strictly natural phenomena. If you choose to live under these sorts of conditions, you will have the added responsibility of protecting your home from these dangers. Another very basic thing would be to check the soil around the house for stability, if you are thinking of living on a mountainside or in the foothills. If the soil is very crumbly and loose, you're asking for trouble. You don't need to be a mystic to figure this out.

A Taoist would not recommend that you live at the very peak of a mountain or very deep down in a sunken knoll, for reasons beyond the obvious ones. *Feng* refers to both Qi and wind. The number-one prohibition in Taoist Feng Shui is this: You should not live in a very windy place. Wind will blow away all the Qi. In order for the Qi to circulate in a healthy way, a gentle breeze is sufficient. No wind at all makes the Qi stagnant, but too much will bring your fortunes down. You can do a simple test to see if a location is too windy. Pour a bucket of water on the ground, and if it dries up very quickly, you know you're in the path of too much wind. Water is money. Excessive wind will blow it away. In the Tao, everything must be in balance. Too much wind should always be avoided.

One thing that you can't have too much of is sunshine. As living beings we are creatures of Yang, but we still have a lot of Yin inside of our bodies. Sixty percent of the human body is composed of water.

This is more than half Yin Qi. This is why we need a lot of sunshine. A large part of Feng Shui and Qi Gong aims at raising our level of energy, for health and spiritual development. Sunlight is the greatest source of living energy available to us. The ancient *Book of Lu* speaks of Ming Ta. The word *Ming* is made from the characters for sun and moon and means "light." *Ta* means "high, wide, spacious." This term conveys the concept of clear seeing in all directions. In Feng Shui, the Ming Ta principle is employed by choosing a home that is not set at a low elevation, that is filled with light, especially morning light, and that is high ceilinged and airy. A house positioned in a gully or depression or with very low ceilings will make you feel stifled, pressured, and squashed down.

It's important to live in an environment that suits your temperament. You must look for a place with the same Qi as you possess, one that will enhance your own level of Qi. "Water is favored by the wise, mountains are favored by the virtuous." Even the look of the house must complement the environment to keep everything flowing together in harmony. If you live down by the ocean, your house should be low slung, not too tall. This is for balance. The house must look calm because the water is quiet. Inside the stillness of the ocean is movement, but to feel its vibration, your energy must be tranquil. You can't see it the same way if you live near a mountain. In this case, the house should be high, rising straight up. The energy is completely different. If you are a quiet, mellow person, this house and location are not for you. For balance, you need to find a proper match.

If you are well-off, that doesn't mean you should have a large house. Some wealthy people feel they must own a mansion to display their riches, but a Taoist Feng Shui master would not recommend this. The size of your home or office must correspond with the number of people living or working in it. Fewer people would mean a smaller house. If there are one or two people working in an office, make it a small office, even if the business is very successful. A small office full of people means a stronger Qi. A big office with only a few people means an insufficient amount of Qi. If a person lives alone in a large house, he or she should get a pet. The amount of living energy needs to coincide with the size of the space, for balance.

All of this can be extended even further to adjust for different people's individual Qi. The sort of people who "fill up a room" with their presence should certainly not be forced to spend a lot of time in a small room, crowded together with many other people. The environment will become unbalanced for everyone involved. According to the Ming Ta principle, just as a place that's too big will create a lack of Qi, a place that's too small will press you down. It is important, then, to have an environment that's light, bright, and airy, and where you have room to stretch. You don't want to feel tightened up. Crossing from a dark entrance hall into a high-ceilinged, open space, you can feel the psychological release. In order to make sense of something, see something to light, realize a project, and make it come true, Ming Ta is the phrase that is used. If you drive a big car, you will have to spend more money on gas, but you will be much safer. It's worth it to allow yourself a spacious living environment, as long as it is within your means. Psychologically, it can help you achieve your goals.

Different personalities require different circumstances. Let's say you are looking for a receptionist. Would you hire someone who is like a wild bird flying free, always on the go? Such a person might really rather be outside than be sitting all day in an office doing paperwork. The job wouldn't be suitable for this person. But someone who has been very sheltered or raised like a bird in a cage would find it very easy to settle down behind a desk.

People sometimes approach Dr. Wu to ask if they can learn acupuncture. If he tells them they are not suitable for it and they hastily protest that they certainly are smart enough to learn, he tells them that with their sharp mind, they should go into business, not acupuncture. The study of acupuncture requires patience and calmness. Taoists have long understood that it takes a long time to change a personality, and that ultimately it is healthier to adjust your surroundings and circumstances to fit the temperament you already have than to force yourself into a situation you may be unable to live up to. Sometimes, the best way to do battle with a dragon is not to go into its cave.

This is why the practice of Feng Shui must always be personally tailored to the individual's needs. Dr. Wu has seen many situations where one family is successful living in a house in which the previous owners did not do as well. When you read the Qi of a place, you must equally be able to assess the Qi of the people you are helping. Like must be put with like. Also, attention must be paid to any special objectives the people may have. If they wish to start a new business, you may need to make adjustments that would not be necessary for someone else whose concerns were primarily health related. In some cases, such as the one involving family with a rock spirit near the backyard pool (described in Chapter 5), the Feng Shui master must balance forces that are helpful and harmful at the same time. All in all, every Feng Shui reading is a unique creation, delicately balanced with the insight of a psychologist and the touch of an artist.

In the Neighborhood

As discussed earlier in the chapter, finding an ideal location for your home or office can be related to the Lords of the Four Directions. Being situated in the middle of the proper blend of mountains, water, trees, and roads, or in a neighborhood with features corresponding to the mountain of the Turtle, the fire of the Bird, the metal of the Tiger, or the water of the Dragon, will transform your house into a special talisman for accumulating Qi. This takes a lot of creative observation, and it may be difficult to find a perfect match. Even Dr. Wu had to make allowances for his own office location. What are some of the most important elements to look for in the environment surrounding your home or office?

First, for an office, notice what sorts of businesses are located nearby. The energy they pull in may be strong enough to affect the Qi of your own place. Obviously, if your house or office has been built over a graveyard, some Yin Qi issues are going to arise. Also, if a previous occupant died in your house, the spirit may still be hovering around. Use the Golden Steel Unbreakable Body exorcism (discussed in Chapter 5) to bring out any potential entities and to neutralize any negative effect they may have. Don't be afraid of these forces. Sometimes they can be helpful.

I accompanied Dr. Wu on a Feng Shui reading of a very spiritual woman's apartment. The moment he entered her home, he went straight for her bedroom and sat down on the bed to meditate. While the rest of us were in the other room chatting, I could sense a palpable shift in the energy of the apartment. After about ten minutes, a pleasant, warm feeling started to fill the room. Afterward, Dr. Wu questioned the woman about how long she had lived in the apartment and whether she lived alone. She had just moved in a few weeks ago and lived by herself. Dr. Wu told her to push her bed over to the wall, because someone had died in that room in a bed that had been positioned in the center, like hers was now. If she didn't give this spirit enough room to move around, it would lay down "on top" of her.

Being psychic herself, the woman told Dr. Wu about what had happened right after she had moved in to the apartment: She saw a ghost appear in her bedroom one night but hadn't thought anything in particular about it. He told her there was no reason to be alarmed, because this ghost, if it had enough room for itself, could actually help her with her new business. All she needed to do was move the bed, keep the bedroom door closed when she wasn't using it, and put a statue of the Buddha on a table by the front door, on an angle in line with her bedroom (fig. 84). Then, her business would gradually increase.

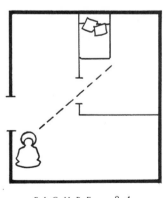

FIGURE. 84

A home or office that is located on top of a burial ground or across the street from a cemetery is more complicated. It's better not to live in a place like this. There is too much Yin Qi to be easily mitigated. If you do live across the street from a cemetery, an eight-trigram mirror hung above your front door might be a temporary solution, but you would simplify your life by moving, if possible. It's also not good to live next to a temple, monastery, or church. In the large Buddhist community in East Los Angeles, many unsuspecting families will try to own homes right next to the Tsi Lai Temple, thinking it will bring holiness to their households. This is a major mistake. The truth is, a family house is Yang and a place of worship is Yin. A church's heavy Yin Qi will harm your home. Your house could also disturb the sanctified silence of the church. It's all right to live in the same area, but keep a respectful distance from places of worship. This is one situation where Yin and Yang do not help each other.

A very beautiful woman mentioned to Dr. Wu that because she was being harassed by so many men asking her for dates, she decided to move right next to the local police department. He told her this was not a good move. Having a police station, fire station, or jail facing your front door, or right behind your property is a source of Ba Qi— aggressive, hostile ("stopped") energy that is a product of strife and struggle. When a bird flies away from you before you are three feet away from it, it is responding to your Ba Qi. Just by living in the modern world, we accumulate Ba Qi. All of us have some. Practicing Qi Gong will help you dissolve the Ba Qi, but this takes work. Why would you want to add fat to the fire by living next to places whose daily work involves this sort of stress and anger? Similarly, living right next to a hospital or mental clinic will radiate sick Qi onto your house. All of these services are necessary to the community, but you don't have to live right next to them to be safe in an emergency.

In contrast, living near a bank or a school is excellent. An elementary school, especially one with kindergartners, is even better than a bank. Remember, children under nine are like water and their Qi is playful and strong. You might think that this location would be too noisy, but it's well worth the ruckus. Children have so much excess Qi that it can emanate up from the school yard and fill your home with vitality. If you move into a new place and find children's drawings scribbled on the walls, don't mind the mess. Those doodles are a good-luck sign for you, and you should examine the messages they contain. I'll never forget when, as a kid, I drew a happy stick person in green crayon on the back windshield of my mother's car. She was never able to scrub it off completely, and she never had an accident in all the years she drove that car. If you move into a house in which previous owners had lived for more than three to five years without having children, there might be something wrong. If you are trying to start a family and are having trouble, you may want to have the Feng Shui checked.

Theaters and restaurants are suitable places to live near. These are lively places where people are enjoying themselves, but the enjoyment is controlled because the people are sitting down. I have a friend who used to live down the block from a big amusement park. During warm summer nights, the screams of the people riding the roller coaster would waft through the open windows. I'm sure they were all having a nice time, but to us, it sounded like the tortures of the damned in the ninth rung of hell. Psychologically, it was very unnerving. Also, the teenagers and the police were always harassing each other. The energy

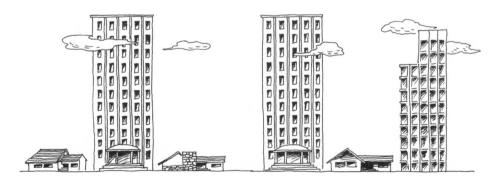

FIGURES. 85 & 86

was just too frenetic. The residents of that block were losing jobs and mortgages and having problems with their kids. Living close to a bus stop, though, is actually not bad. The busses come and go with passengers, dropping some off, taking new ones on. The energy in all this coming and going can help bring the life force to your home.

The size of your house or office in relation to the surrounding buildings is also an important consideration. If your building is the only tall one around, will be out of line with the general flow of the Qi. The same holds for a building that is small and hemmed in on each side by tall buildings. Living right next to a high-rise building or on the bottom floor of one is not good. All the good Feng Shui will be taken away by the taller buildings (figs. 85 and 86).

Right now, I live in a situation like this. I have a small bungalow in a large yard, but it is surrounded by two- and three-storey apartment buildings. Fortunately for me, there is a huge old pepper tree at the back of my yard that reaches taller than the surrounding buildings. I can feel it shielding my Qi, like a protective canopy, preventing my home from having too sunken or squeezed of an energy. I also have a number of tall pine and banana trees that bal-

FIGURE. 87

ance out old "grandma" from being too overpowering. Even so, it has never been easy for me to work out of my home, which is why I keep a separate office and studio for my business (fig. 87).

It's always best for your house to be the first house on the block or to be located squarely in the middle of your block. The Qi is best focused on these two positions. You don't want to be at the tail end of the block (in order of street number), for all that it implies. You need to be very careful about having the corners of surrounding buildings pointing at you. As discussed in Chapter 6, these angles send out penetrating lines of harsh Qi toward your house. If a hostile corner is pointing at your front door, it can be held back by burying clear crys-

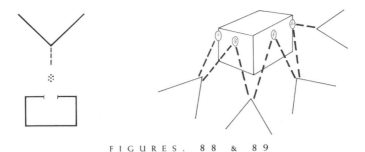

tals (round or diamond shaped) or animal shells in the 3 Mountain formation or the 7 formation. You can use any type of shell—clam, oyster,
or turtle, for example. The crystals are placed five feet from your front
door pointing back at the harsh angle (fig. 88).

The more corners facing your home or office, the more trouble-
some the problem becomes. To resolve it, you can use mirrors in conjunction with wind chimes. Place them in between the multiple hard
angles. The chimes must have five tones and the mirrors should be positioned high up on the walls. In this case, you can also hang feathers
and/or pictures of any of the animals of the Chinese zodiac. Talismans
can be buried, as yet another option (fig. 89).

If your house is faced by a corner that has been flattened off, this
is not a problem. Even if the building is larger than yours, no measures
need to be taken because no penetrating line is being formed (fig. 90).
However, if someone's chimney is facing your front door, hang a regular flat mirror above the door frame to reflect it back. Fire burns away

F I G U R E S . 9 0 & 9 1

water, and your fortunes could go up in smoke (fig. 91).

A more difficult situation to remedy is when your house is being blocked or obstructed by another (fig. 92). When women are having trouble getting pregnant, the first thing Dr. Wu asks them is if another house is blocking theirs.

FIGURE. 92

Electromagnetic radiation from electrical poles and the like within 50 feet from your house can be remedied with a porcelain rooster pointing beak first out of your window at the poles. Roosters can at times also help harsh angles if the window placements on the abutting building visually cue that "centipede" look.

If your office is located in a multistoried building, it's important to know what type of businesses are operating directly above yours. For example, Dr. Wu did the Feng Shui for a banking office that was downstairs from a health spa. This was not a good location, because the dirty, outgoing water of the spa's showers and steam rooms was being flushed downward over the bank. He advised the clients to move their office or convince the spa owners to relocate. Any other Feng Shui placement would be a stopgap for this "draining" situation.

The Street Where You Live

It's important for your house to be on level ground, even if you are considering a house in the hills (fig. 93). It is acceptable for your home to be on a slight incline, but you should avoid any plots of land that rise sharply up or plunge steeply down (figs. 94 through 96) This placing is important on all sides of your house—the front,

FIGURE. 93

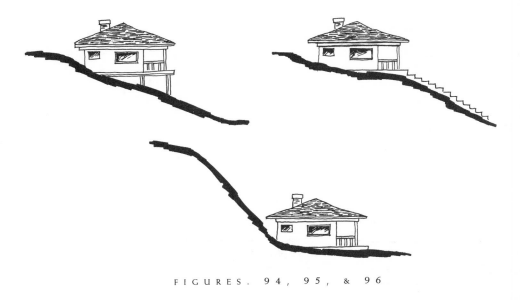

FIGURES. 94, 95, & 96

back, and sides. This also holds true for your driveway or the street your house is located on. Going up too steep of a slope day in and day out will contribute to a feeling of always climbing, working too hard, never getting to the top. You want the surface of your driveway and the street approaching your house to be smooth, without serious potholes or bumps, for the same reason. Dr. Wu did the Feng Shui for a house right on the beach near San Diego. The house's Feng Shui was good and it's position facing the ocean was excellent, but the road leading to it was so bumpy that it brought the entire level of the energy way down. A very bumpy road will siphon off one's wealth.

The best type of street to be located on is one that gently curves and winds like an S (fig. 97). A perfectly straight thoroughfare is not as good (fig. 98). If it is straight, it should at least have some mild slopes that take you up and down a bit (fig. 99). Living on a boulevard or a very wide, busy street is also bad. The Qi rushes by your house too quickly. This also holds true for living near a freeway, highway, or bridge. These positions should always be avoided (fig. 100).

If two streets come to a point directly opposite your front door,

FIGURES. 97, 98, 99, & 100

you need to bury a 3-Mountain crystal talisman. You need to use dia-mond-shaped crystals, not spherical ones. In this case, you can also use wood, metal, rocks, or nails. Bury the talisman five feet from your front door, pointing back at the juncture in the road (fig. 101). If you have to break up the sidewalk to bury your crystals, it must be done. The house I grew up in had a configuration similar to this, and even with traffic lights on the corner less than a block up, every one of the four houses on that inter-section had at one time or another been crashed into by out-of-control cars (fig. 102). In our case, a whole patio wall was knocked clear through. If your house is located on a spot either in front or behind this sort of fork, it is not safe.

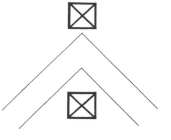

FIGURE. 101

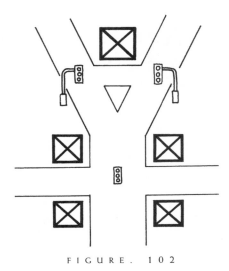

FIGURE. 102

Another very dangerous street position is called "running into the road." In this situation, your home or office stands right at the head of a road (fig. 103). Dr. Wu had warned the owners of a local shop to move their store out of a location that was like this. They scoffed, saying they were at the top of an uphill grade. No one would possibly be able to come barreling up a hill. Unfortunately, just a couple of months later, a drunk driver did just that, hitting and killing the store owner's wife. Tragedy could have been averted if they had listened to Dr. Wu.

A house on a center island between two or more cross streets is also in a bad location (fig. 104). Being in a location with obvious traffic hazards will put a house at risk of misfortune. Another arrangement that operates on the same principle but that is less obvious to the eye is called the "bow and arrow street." When the arrow is stretched over the bow or curve of a road, pointing directly at your house, you and your family are at great risk (fig. 105). This position applies to cul-de-sacs and other types of semicircular streets (figs. 106 through 108). If your house is located in one of these positions, there will be no way to

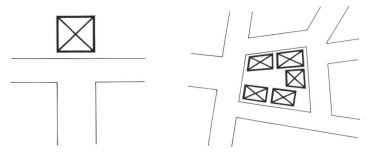

FIGURES. 103 & 104

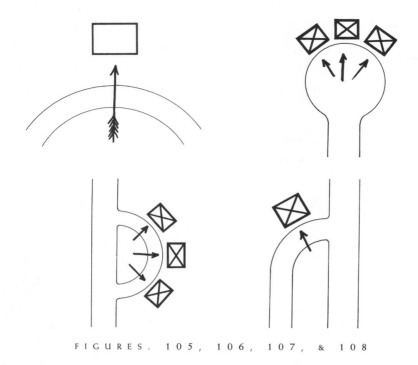

prosper. Even if you are already well-off, your children or grandchildren could lose their wealth.

Quite often, a large house will have a semicircular driveway in front of it (fig. 109). This is also considered a "bow and arrow" position. The marriage may end in divorce, separation, or even untimely death.

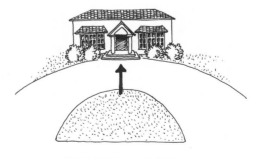

FIGURE. 109

Dr. Wu estimates that there is a 90 percent chance of marital problems and divorce resulting from having this sort of driveway. Do everything in your power to reconfigure a driveway, car port, or walkway that faces your house in this semicircular way.

The Shape of Your House

In the Tao it is said, the sky is a circle and the earth is a square—Tian Yuan Di Feng. "The sky is a circle" (Tian Yuan) means your house should have a comfortably high ceiling. Too low-ceilinged a place will make you feel impacted or pressurized. "The earth is a square" (Di Feng) means your house must be square. In Beijing, the Summer Palace contains eighty-one houses and halls, and each hall and each room in each hall is perfectly square. The ideal of a square house with a high ceiling is also expressed in the Ming Ta principle, with *Ta* meaning "regular and spacious." A square is the symbol of peace.

A square house or office contains the Qi in a way that is closest to nature. A rectangular house is not as good. Houses with five or six (or more) sides are not uncommon in contemporary architecture, but they can create many Feng Shui problems, not the least of which is the creation of many "hostile" angles (fig.110). The more square your house or apartment is, the better it will be for you. A house that is wide in the front and narrow toward the rear is called a "coffin house" (fig.

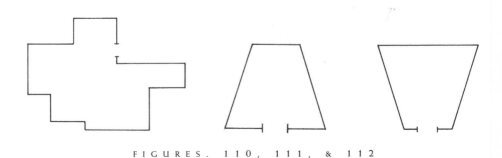

FIGURES. 110, 111, & 112

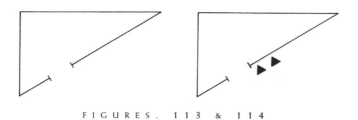

FIGURES. 113 & 114

111). This is not beneficial. From the outside the house might look large and grand, but once you enter it, you will find yourself facing down a vanishing perspective with nowhere to run to. However, a house that is narrow in the front and wide in the back is quite good (fig. 112). It means you will store up a lot of wealth.

A house with an angle missing, having only three sides, can affect fertility (fig. 113). A patient of Dr. Wu's had been trying to get pregnant for a long time. Western doctors blamed her condition on an autoimmune deficiency, which is often used as a catch-all phrase when nothing else wrong can be found. Artificial insemination didn't work, nor did seeing other Chinese doctors. When the woman finally arrived at Dr. Wu's clinic, he suggested that he take a look at her house. It had a triangular shape. He told her to buy two purple mountain (amethyst) crystals and bury them next to her front door (fig. 114). Amethyst crystals are always used in pairs. Two months later, the woman was pregnant. This is the power of Feng Shui. Again, there is no medical explanation for this amazing turn of events. There are things out there beyond the grasp of logic.

One type of structure you should under no circumstances spend more than a night or two in is a pyramid. The pyramid is a Yin house, good Feng Shui only for a tomb. If you live in a house with this shape, you will die or have a nervous breakdown. It has proportions that block the light of life.

I had a strange lesson in the influence of the pyramid. One day, after having developed my senses to a certain point, I was driving on a busy freeway interchange, just past downtown L.A. Looking ahead, I

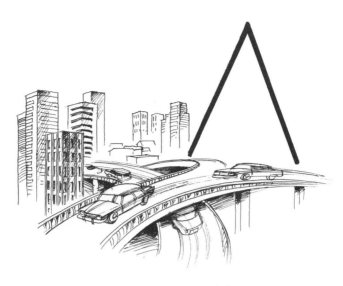

saw a tremendous blue pyramid looming a thousand feet into the sky, towering over the junction of the overpass (fig. 115). The more I looked at it, the more solid it became. I felt it must be some sort of emanation that coexisted with that spot on another plane. As I got closer, I saw a bad accident had taken place up ahead.

The next time I drove by that spot, the pyramid was still there, and it continued to be there every time I happened to pass. I finally asked Dr. Wu about it and he confirmed what I had been suspecting— that it was a very dangerous location and the pyramid was standing as a marker of it. He suggested that I avoid the interchange as much as possible. It wasn't safe. Strangely enough, a year later, I came across a reproduction of a rare Tibetan devotional painting depicting the offerings to the Lords of the Underworld. Looming large in its black landscape was a blue pyramid, the same color and shape of the one I had seen.

At the time, Dr. Wu also recommended that I put a bird or some bird feathers in my car for protection. This I found even more amazing because it made me recall the first car I owned. For years I drove it with a plastic parrot on a perch hanging from the rearview mirror, as a campy little decoration, but not once in all that time did I get into an accident. Then, the car was stolen, parrot and all, and within two weeks of driving my new car, I was rear-ended by a tractor trailer. A bird in your car (even a fake one) really works.

The forces of Yin can be of great help to us as warnings of potential danger, but since there's already enough Yin around, we should be careful about encouraging it to proliferate around the house. Therefore, whenever you do Feng Shui, you must know exactly where all the water is. Look first at the kitchen, then at the bathrooms, and always carefully check all possible water sources around the outside of the house. When Dr. Wu reads a house's Feng Shui, he tries to find the location of the water. If he finds nothing obvious, like a stream or a swimming pool, he looks for the plumbing underground. You need to know exactly where the water is and the direction of its flow.

As we've said many times in this book, water is your fortune. It must always be moving and circulating. Still water is a major problem. If your family is sick all the time, or if strange, unexplainable occurrences happen often, check to see if there are any small holes or shallow depressions around your house. The same thing holds for an office. If you find any pits within five feet of the front door, fill them up with dirt.

If there is an extreme sense of uneasiness, make sure there isn't a dry well somewhere nearby. If there is, fill it up. This isn't scientifically proven, but in Dr. Wu's experience, if there is a ghost about, there must be a well or a hollow place that is impure. Swimming pools can be problematic, as well. Remember the Green Dragon, and try to keep it on the left side of your house. Adverse Ling energy from rocks, trees, and so forth needs the help of water to arise. Lots of things cannot be explained. They just come up for no reason. Taoist exorcism can help you to see the problems, but sometimes to keep them at bay, you will need to apply Xiong Huang wine. This is what the family with the rock spirit placed around the pool as an extra measure of precaution.

Xiong Huang wine is a special tincture of powdered ore, namely realgar, mixed with wine that is used to hold back ghosts and force them to leave. Its invention is attributed to Lao Tze, and its use dates back to the Tang Dynasty. The Tang emperor, Li Shi Min, had put to death his faithful general, who had been falsely implicated in a palace intrigue. Afterward, the emperor was beset with horrible nightmares of his dead general, pointing at him accusingly, night after sleepless night. The imperial doctor, Sun Ze Miao, sprinkled Xiong Huang wine in the four corners of the royal bed to help remove the general's restless soul.

Xiong Huang wine is prepared according to a secret Taoist ritual. The metal ores are smelted in an eight-trigram cauldron, which must be sealed tightly against all evaporation and then buried in the ground in a special location. There, it must remain for eighty-one days, after which a ceremony must accompany its removal from the earth. The powder that is left is mixed with liquor and is said to have many protective qualities.

To this day, country people apply this mixture before a long trip or when having to work late at night to gain courage. Xiong Huang wine can be used around the perimeter of a swimming pool to keep ghostly Ling energies from arising. It can also be placed in the four corners of the bathroom for purification. It can even be applied to the wheels of a car at noon on the ninth day of the ninth month of the Chinese Lunar calendar to ensure safety on the road. Its spirit-chasing properties last for seven years, after which time, it must be reapplied. Yet again, the art of Taoist Feng Shui touches upon realms of magic that have been shut out of the modern world, but that still hold remarkable importance for our lives.

8

Inside the Space

The purpose of Feng Shui is to locate problems, turn them into benefits, and thus bring fortune to your life. There are special implications for your health and wealth located within your home or office. Just as outside, inside the home the Feng Shui practitioner seeks to cleanse and energize the Qi, directing its flow to stimulate desired goals. In many ways, adjusting the inside of your home is the most critical phase of this process. Qi comes down from the heavens and up from the earth, merges into the environment that surrounds your house, and finally flows in and out of its interior. As the home is the center of our daily lives, having the right balance of Qi there is vital for our happiness and success. The most personal and private moments of our lives are spent inside—eating, spending time with friends and family, taking care of bodily needs, and most importantly, sleeping. Without healthy Feng Shui inside our homes, we will become vulnerable during these private times, which can carry over into our more public lives.

Finding the Center

The season and place of your birth determine the center of your life. Any exploration or search for success moves outward from these points. As discussed in Chapter 2, if you were born in the spring, heading east from your hometown will lead you toward your fortunes. Just as life has a center starting point, so does your house. For proper Feng Shui, the Qi of your home must be flowing outward, to help you get "out" where you need to be. Once you have determined the exact center of your house or apartment, you will know the primal source of your personal Qi. All of the energy in your life radiates out from this point.

"Finding the center" is a fundamental concept in Taoist Feng Shui. It may sound very fancy, but finding the center is really very simple. Just locate the spot in the dead-center of your house. If it helps to visualize it, draw a floor plan and then draw diagonal lines from the corners. The point where the lines intersect will be your center point (fig. 116).

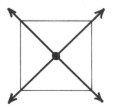 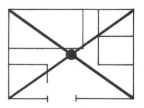

FIGURES. 116 & 117

Now it is easy to understand why a perfectly square house is best (fig. 117). It may have hallways and rooms positioned in an irregular way, but there are only two main lines of energy coming from the house's outer corners. They divide the house into equally balanced sections, creating harmony and stability.

Remember, corners and angles create lines of Qi. Too many of these can start to pile up, one energy pathway on top of another, until things start getting chaotic. Look at how many lines of Qi develop from a simple L-shaped house (fig. 118). All of these crossing angles would have to be eased with crystals or other talismans in order to calm down the Qi of this house. As you can guess, doing all of this can become rather complicated. Even in a rectangular house, the sectors surrounding the center point are uneven (fig. 119). A weakened center point, caused by an odd-shaped house or a house whose original dimensions have been significantly altered (by adding rooms, bay windows, a partial second floor), can destabilize the nervous system and possibly increase the chances of mental exhaustion and collapse. If you and your spouse get sick a lot, chances are the center point of your house is weak.

What should you do if your house has an irregular shape? To simplify things, you can locate a main center point by completing the square on your floor plan (fig. 120). As can be seen from the diagrams, this won't change the fact that your focus point is in a weak position, but at least now you will know exactly where you need to shore it up.

If you are trying to find the center point of an apartment or office, you will probably encounter a situation wherein the exact center is

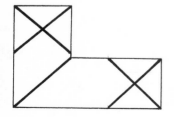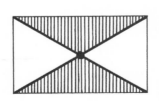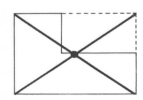

FIGURES. 118, 119, & 120

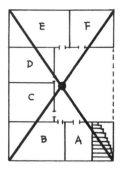

FIGURE. 1 2 1

impossible to locate. In these cases, then, you want to judge how closely located your unit is to the center point of the floor (fig. 121). In the diagram, for example, Unit D's front door is closest to the center. This unit would be the best apartment on this floor. The farther a unit is from the center of the floor, the worse it will be for you. In the example, Office A would be the worst unit. Even though Units A and B are farthest from the center, Unit A is worse because it's also closer to the blank areas of the hall and stairwell. There needs to be plenty of human Qi at the center point. The worst type of building is one that has an empty courtyard in its center. If there is a flower bed or tree in the middle of the courtyard, you should forget about having anything to do with this place. It will make you flat broke.

The Bedroom

What should be at the center point? If you know the center point of your home is weak, the best remedy is to reposition the master bedroom at this spot. Using the largest bedroom in the house is, by far, the surest way to make the center point heavier and stronger. If a couple is sick a lot, the problem is usually a bedroom that is too small. We sleep for approximately a third of our lives. At night, when we are at rest, our bodies go into action, repairing the wear and tear that the organ networks received during the day. The environment of the bedroom must be carefully arranged to create the most conducive atmosphere for restful sleeping and healing.

The first priority in the bedroom is plenty of fresh air. The master bedroom should be the largest room in the house, especially if you are not well or your spouse is not well. Move your bedroom to the biggest room, taking over the living room, the rec room, or whichever room is largest. This is of primary importance. You will receive the best air flow and the largest amount of oxygen if your bedroom is large. For this reason, you shouldn't keep cut flowers or have a fireplace in the bedroom. Also, there should be air circulation underneath your bed, so keep that space completely clear—no storage, nothing dirty, no shoes, no bins or suitcases. Suitcases should never be out in plain view in your house, in any case. They might make you feel like you have to move. The only thing you want under your bed is the lucky seven-crystal talisman. Form it out of crystals, glass marbles, piles of rice, beans, coins, or anything else that will symbolize the accumulation of Qi and wealth.

When you are asleep, you are most vulnerable to outside influences. If they are fortunate, like the seven-crystal talisman, you will absorb their good vibrations; but if they are negative, they will affect you more strongly than in any other room in the house. Dr. Wu once did the Feng Shui for a single woman who had previously had it done by another practitioner. She was advised at that time to hang a red cloth over the headboard of her bed. Dr. Wu told her that this red cloth was for getting rid of evil spirits. Positioned like it was over her bed, it was not only keeping the ghosts away, but was also getting rid of all the potential men that wanted to come to her. It was blocking their way. He told her to move the red cloth to a spot under the bed, where it would still do her some good while not causing problems at the same time.

Mirrored sliding closet doors in the bedroom are not good. Taoists use mirrors to confront and repulse evil. When you are asleep, you don't want to be facing a mirror. Over the long term, this will ruin your health. Mirrors are supposed to face ghosts and trap them. If the mirrors face you, they will trap your energy instead. If you have large mirrors in the bed-

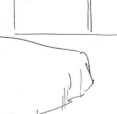

FIGURE. 122

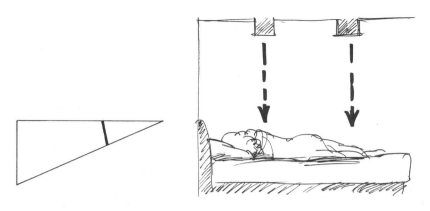

FIGURES. 123 & 124

room, you can angle track lights onto them (fig. 122). Keep the lights on timers so you can fall asleep with them still on. This is only a temporary measure, though. In the long run, you should have all mirrors removed from the bedroom.

The bedroom door should not line up with the front door. In addition, the bedroom ought to be as square as possible. At the very least, it should have four corners. Triangular bedrooms will cause fertility problems. If you have a triangular bedroom, try putting up a partition across one of the angles (fig. 123). You will then have four corners. Your bedroom should not be too narrow. A narrow bedroom will create feelings of loneliness that could lead to marital discord or divorce. Also avoid exposed ceiling beams when at all possible. If you have a beamed ceiling in your bedroom, make sure your bed is placed parallel to them. You don't want a bed and a ceiling beam to cross (fig. 124). This situation would be like two cars crashing into one another. It would also be detriment to your health and career. If this situation cannot be avoided, hand 5 small, round, multifaceted crystals from the beam over the bed to disperse its pressurizing energy.

Recently, Dr. Wu treated a patient with chronic, debilitating migraine headaches. After months of treatment, her condition had only slightly improved. He believed her physical condition was mostly normal, so he suggested a Feng Shui reading. In her bedroom, he found a small hole in the wall by her bed. This is what was causing her headaches. The patient wondered how such a small hole could create such a big problem. The draft coming in through the crack, called a "thief wind," was working on the same principle as a gun. The longer the barrel, the farther the bullet is shot. Compress the space around the bullet as it is being shot, and it will be expelled with much greater intensity. The narrowness of the hole had condensed the force of the draft. The patient plastered it up, and within a week her migraines were almost completely gone. If there are any cracks in your bedroom walls or ceiling, fill them in immediately. If you follow this outline for a healthy bedroom, you will be amazed at how much it will improve the quality of your sleeping, and waking, hours.

The Living Room

The bedroom is the most important room in the house for your health. If you don't have your health, you really don't have anything. This is why a proper bedroom works best in the center point of your house. Alternately, your living room or dining room can be located in the center. This will bring prosperity. Having these rooms as the focus of your house will maximize the happy times spent there with family and friends. If your dining room is in the center, place the dining table in the middle of the room, perhaps with a nice, bright chandelier hanging above it. Use a tablecloth in the color of your birth season for even more emphasis.

If your living room is in the center, make sure it has plenty of sunlight and fresh air. A fireplace is fine, but don't put your family photos on the mantelpiece. Obviously, this is a bad choice given that our bodies are 60 percent water. Iron fireplace accessories or other metal objects are good to have around the hearth. Metal and fire go together. Always keep wood inside the fireplace, even if you never light it. And of course, don't have any water or water-related items nearby.

Some people like to keep a shrine out of respect to their ancestors. If you have one, keep it away from the fireplace and keep it at eye level. These are signs of respect. An average table will be too low. A shrine should not be placed in the center of the house, which should be reserved for the living. Don't keep religious statues or alters in the same room as your ancestors' shrine. These objects carry a very different kind of energy. Even when practicing Qi Gong, the points in the forms that honor one's ancestors and one's god are kept clearly separated.

If you keep pictures of spiritual masters hanging on the wall, they must be of teachers over sixty years of age. If your masters died young, there was a karmic reason for this. It had nothing to do with the purity of their teachings, but if they did not live long enough to reach the level of cultivation that only age can confer, their images should not be on your wall. Instead, keep their pictures tucked into your cherished books. In Taoism, putting a picture inside of a book is a way of creating an eternal memorial. Invite your younger teachers out on holidays, for special occasions, and for ceremonies of thanks. You will not dishonor them by not keeping their pictures hung up. It's just better for the living to keep pictures of only the older, long-lived masters on the wall.

The Kitchen

When inspecting someone's Feng Shui, look at the state of the kitchen first, before any other room in the house. The kitchen is the kingdom of incoming water. As we have said repeatedly, inflowing water is the clear, health-giving water that represents your money and luck. Also, the kitchen represents the balance of Yin and Yang. It is the one place in the house where it is natural and acceptable to have both fire and water. But there should always be some distance between the bedroom and the kitchen. If you have an infant, do not keep a hot plate in the bedroom for making warm bottles at night. There should never be any

F I G U R E S .   1 2 5 ,   1 2 6 ,   &   1 2 7

cooking or fire in the bedroom. This combination of fire and water must be strictly contained in the kitchen.

    If the woman of the house is frequently
sick, the problem is in the kitchen. The refrigerator and the stove are not properly placed or
are too close together. In the kitchen, the
refrigerator needs to be in the north and the
stove in the south (fig. 125). North is the birth-
place of water and south is the home of fire.
Alternately, the stove can be in the east and the
refrigerator in the west. If the appliances are
too close together, remedy the problem by

covering the side of the refrigerator that is touching the stove with aluminum foil. This will also help with splashing oil. If you don't do much
frying, you can instead hang a tortoise shell or three feathers across the
width of the refrigerator (figs. 126 and 127).

    If your gas stove hookup is not positioned on the south side of the
kitchen, keep a hot plate, an electric wok, or something else that gets
hot there instead. If a stove cannot be moved from its position in the
north, cover it with shiny silver aluminum foil and hang a mirror above
it. Putting cold or watery objects like a water cooler around the stove
is a trickier proposition. If the water cooler is big enough, it will work;

but if the cooler is even slightly too small, it will stimulate the imbalance even further. Remember, fire and water fight against each other, but when that perfect balance is achieved, it can suddenly create a brand new Qi from the ashes of the old. This is among the most profound applicationa of Taoist Feng Shui.

The Bathroom

Being aware of incoming and outgoing water is a necessity. You need to be very careful not to mix the two. For example, don't keep a washing machine in the kitchen or hand-wash clothes in the kitchen sink. You don't want any dirty water in the kitchen, where only clean, incoming water should be. The main location of dirty water is the bathroom. In the past, this wasn't as much of a problem as it is today, with our modern conveniences right inside the home. Now, we have to be extra careful about every aspect of the bathroom. Most importantly, it must be spotlessly clean—the cleanest room in the house. Otherwise, money will never accumulate. The Taoist saying, "Two eyes above, two eyes below," compares the importance of the eyes with the anus and urethra. These four openings of the body must be exposed to wholesomeness and purity. In other words, scrub the bathroom as frequently as you brush your teeth or wash your hands.

Make sure there are no books, papers, or dirty clothes on the bathroom floor. Also keep it smelling clean. In Chinese medicine, it is considered easier to treat a patient who is clean than one who is not clean. If the patient has a strong odor of soy sauce rising from the body, it could indicate that an illness is deeply rooted in the patient's system. Putting some Xiong Huang wine in the four corners of the bathroom is always a helpful touch. The object of all this is to prevent your health and wealth from being flushed down the drain.

Generally, if all members of your family are sick all the time, the bathroom is in the wrong place. It should be in a corner or on one side of the house. It must never be right in the center of the house. A bathroom in this spot has the power to break a family apart. Also, when you open your front door, you should not be able to see a bathroom. This placement is a bad thing that worsens over time. If your toilet faces north or northeast, you need to do something to correct this problem. Having the plumbing moved could cost thousands of dollars, which is not something most people can afford. Alternately, you can hang a mirror on the wall, square or round, opposite the toilet to reflect it back on itself. You can also use a crystal ball in the same position. Faucets and shower heads should absolutely never point southeast or southwest. This will create a Ghost Line. Fix the problem by installing swiveling faucets and shower nozzles that can be twisted into a different direction. (For more on the Ghost Line, see Chapter 6.)

All these specifications for bathrooms generally apply to office bathrooms as well. But you are better off not having a toilet right in the office. Even though a faucet in the home represents incoming money, in an office, a sink is a major mistake. All water in an office is considered outflowing. Instead of gaining wealth, you will lose it down the drain.

Hallways and Storage

The hallways of a home or office always need some attention because they tend to create all sorts of problems in the flow of Qi. They can break up the space, be dark or dim, and, by their shape, force the Qi to flow in a direction that may not be ideal for you. If the parents and children in a family are having trouble getting along, the problem is very frequently due to the hallway.

First and foremost, keep your hallways clean and clear. Don't keep a lot of things stored in a hallway. Bookshelves, clothes racks, laundry

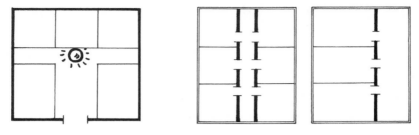

bins, and the like all take up room in a space that should always feel free and unconstricted. If you have a hallway running the length of your house, from the front door to the back, it forms the configuration of "a road running into the house" discussed in Chapter 7. Hang a crystal ball or mirror up at the end of the hall to correct the problem (fig. 128).

A layout that has doors facing each other along the length of a hallway should be avoided. It's much better to have the doors on only one side of the hall (fig. 129). This holds true especially in office buildings and apartment houses, where strangers are living and working opposite each other. Unless you take measures to counteract the problem, you will encounter disputes and arguments between the tenants whose doors directly face each other across the hall. Hang feathers, turtle shells, and the like on your door. In one case involving a woman whose house had two bathrooms on opposite sides of the same hallway, one for her children and one for her tenant, Dr. Wu recommended that she close one of them up. Failing that, their doors should always be kept shut, and preferably, one bathroom be used only for washing the hands.

In your home or office, the northern side represents human relationships, and the southern side represents peaceful, stable working conditions. These two directions should not be used for storage space or garbage. If you do have closets in these directions, and you have no other options, do try to keep them as neat, clean, and free from accumulated junk as you can. I have this situation in my house, and I can attest to the fact that keeping them very pared down makes an enormous difference. It seems like such a small thing, but it makes a big change in the energy of the atmosphere.

Be very careful where you keep your trash cans. If trash cans or dumpsters are kept in the front, it will harm the Qi of your home or building. Having them on the side is not much better. Keep garbage receptacles at the back of the house. Also, don't keep any refuse or piles of leaves or wood in the center of your backyard. This is not good, either.

Incoming and Outgoing Qi

In Taoist Feng Shui, as we have seen, much importance is given to the coming in and going out of energy. It can bring in many fortunate opportunities or whisk them away, depending on the position of your home or office. The Qi of an office must be flowing inward. You want business to pour in. The energy of a home must be flowing outward. You want to get out and accomplish things. Dr. Wu has a friend who lives in a farm-style apartment. Her open kitchen, which is the first thing you see upon entering, has its own miniature beams and shingled roof. This was not good. Having a false "house" within her house would keep her inside, preventing her from achieving her goals. She put a crystal ball and a flowing fountain on the counter facing the door, so they became the first things that could be seen when entering the apartment. She has had to work hard, but things are beginning to turn around for her.

Be extra careful when getting the directions of your house or office situated. If you get this principle mixed up, it will mess up the Qi and cause you to have a lot of problems. You need to go with the flow. As discussed in Chapter 2, use your birth date to determine which

FIGURES. 130 & 131

direction your living and working spaces must face. For example, if you were born in the summer, your best direction is south. For a home, your house or apartment would have to be situated in the north and, when standing inside the house looking out, the front door would have to face south. As you leave your home, you want to be moving in a southerly direction (fig. 130). For an office or business, though, you would want to have customers and money coming in through the front door. Therefore, when they approach your building, they must be coming southwards into your shop. Your office must be in the south, with its front door pointing north, to achieve this effect (fig. 131).

The importance of this concept cannot be overemphasized. Again, my own personal experience bore the truth of this matter out. My birth direction is east; I was born in the spring. My house is on the west side of town and my front door faces east. This is a perfect setup for my home environment. Unfortunately, for a year I was out of a studio due to earthquake damage. To save money, I set up my office in my home. It turned out to be the most sluggish year my business ever had. Many promising deals I had on tap before the move just fizzled out like wet matches, and all sorts of situations cropped up that wound up costing me more than I had saved. Once my studio was moved back to its original location—with its entrance facing west—things picked right up.

That year wasn't a total failure, however. I started finding new opportunities and career directions the further I got from my usual work; I was flowing eastward out of my house to discover new areas of my life opening up. As far as anything coming into my home that was related to the work I had there, it was a complete bust. No matter how much effort I put into it, some obstruction always arose. Now that the Qi flows east into my studio, my creative juices are up and all the old projects are back on. Do not overlook this crucial aspect of Feng Shui.

The idea of incoming and outgoing Qi also plays a role for the family garage. If you find you are tired all the time, your garage may be improperly positioned. If the garage door faces the direction opposite to your birth season, it's not good. Like your house, your garage must align with the outgoing Qi. Inside the garage, put up a mirror to reflect back on the car, to make the Qi flow in the right direction. Or hang a wind chime on the outside corner of the garage that corresponds to your direction. You will soon start feeling much more energetic. If both you and your spouse feel tired but have different birth directions, go with the direction of the spouse who is the breadwinner of the family. If you both make equal amounts of money or share a business together, flip a coin.

There are a few other points to remember when checking your directions for incoming and outgoing Qi. If your property has a number of buildings on it, check the direction of the front door belonging to the main house. If you are located in a large building with many other offices or apartments, go by the direction of your own front door, not the entrance to the building.

The only exception to this rule comes into play in tall buildings with more than five floors. If your office or apartment is located on the first to fifth floor of the building, use the front door to determine

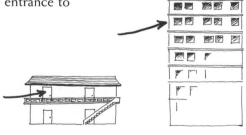

FIGURE. 132

the direction. If it is located above the fifth floor, check the directions of the windows in the unit to determine the direction in which your home or business is facing (fig. 132). For example, one man's previous office was on the second floor of his building. His birth direction being north, his front door faced south and the Qi flowed into his office in a northerly direction. But then he moved to a new office located on the ninth floor of a high-rise building. He made sure to take an office on the south side of the building so that all of his windows would face south. All the Qi coming in from outside again flowed in a northerly direction through his office windows. Because the new office was on the ninth floor, the direction of the Qi flowing into his front door was irrelevant. Above five stories, the windows represent the front door. This is key information. Again, if you get this mixed up, you will make a basic Feng Shui mistake, one that you will come to regret. Learning to go with the flow is the basic truth of Taoist Feng Shui.

Miscellaneous Building Elements

Certain layouts in a home or office are particularly bad and should be avoided at all cost. They direct the Qi in ways that even the most skillful Feng Shui practitioner cannot do much to improve. Four or more rooms opening onto one another with their doors aligned in a straight row, all in one direction, is very bad (fig. 133). This is called "three doors going through your heart." The only thing that can be done to remedy this situation is to wall up the doors and knock out new ones that face in different directions. Rooms leading to rooms leading to still other rooms are never good for the home or office. Unless something is done, sooner or later problems will arise.

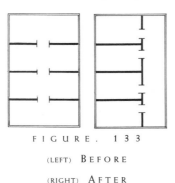

FIGURE. 133

(LEFT) BEFORE

(RIGHT) AFTER

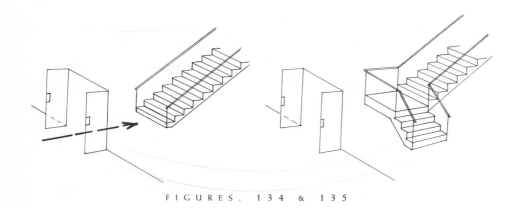

Even worse than "three doors going through your heart" is having a staircase directly facing the front door (fig. 134). You must never live or work in a situation like this. It is the biggest Feng Shui problem you could possibly have. Even if a hallway or an entrance room is between the stairs and the front door, the situation is still bad. Sudden troubles will occur without any forewarning. Misfortune will just come unexpectedly. Generally, this position will make you fail all the time. This must be believed. You have to take steps to fix this problem or move. Build a few extra stairs at the bottom and add a railing, curving the direction of the stairwell away from the front door (fig. 135). This will make it much better. Stairs facing a wall are all right. If your home has this problem, you must find a way to resolve it, or it will cause serious trouble.

In all his years of practicing Feng Shui, Dr. Wu has never once seen this situation not bring a sudden change of affairs. The seriousness of this problem cannot be emphasized enough. In his many years of Feng Shui analysis, Dr. Wu has seen many sudden tragic events occur in homes that had not fixed this positioning. Even Dr. Wu himself was not impervious to this condition. In a previous office, the building had stairs facing the front door. Before moving in, he took special steps to secure his own suite. Years went by, and Dr. Wu's office was the only one in the whole building that didn't change hands. Also, many of the tenants had accidents and broken bones. Even still, the clinic finally had to move on short notice. Feng Shui can remedy many conditions, but this is one that even the best informed adjustments cannot change. As we have said before, the Feng Shui master can help your car take a detour on the road of life, but in the end, you must always arrive at your destination.

These are the two worst Feng Shui problems you could possibly encounter. There are others that, while sometimes challenging, can usually be fixed. For instance, all doors, especially the front door, should be easy to open. They should not be blocked by any obstructions. The layout of your room must go in the same direction as the door. Low cupboards facing the door, for example, disrupt the flow of Qi as you enter a room. They drag the eye downward, and their constant opening and shutting will trap the Qi. When Dr. Wu did a Feng Shui reading of the China Airlines building, the first thing he noticed was a circular bank of receptionists in the lobby. He told the building's owners that he didn't need to see anything else; this was their problem. He advised them to rearrange the circle of receptionists into a straight line. In the circular position, each receptionist's energy was constantly crashing into another's, like airplane disasters. Sitting straight ahead in a row focused the flow of energy and aligned it with the purpose of the business (fig. 136). Now, business is good.

A house or office building with a grand facade and entrance room leading to narrow corridors and small, low-ceilinged rooms is not good.

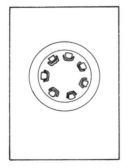 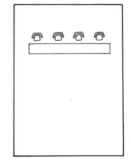

FIGURE. 136

The psychological reaction to the space is not healthy. Day after day, this will contribute to a feeling of being trapped and squeezed, with no escape. Another condition that leads to a trapped feeling is a home or office with no back door or window. Our inner defense mechanisms require the assurance that there is always a way out. Sun Tzu discusses the many permutations of this condition in *The Art of War*. In particular, people over the age of fifty who are starting out in a new business must have a door or window in the back.

Having too many doors or windows is not good, either. One window per room is enough. Ideally, you want your windows to face east and to be high enough to catch the sunlight, but not so high that you can't see out of them. East-facing windows are the best ones for your home. If you don't have at least one, you should build one in. Having two windows directly opposite each other is not good. All your Qi and luck will go in one end and out the other. North-facing windows are very dangerous. North is water. Having open windows in the north can make you lose your wealth. If you have one in your house, you should seal it up right away. I did an informal poll of people I know whose homes had been burglarized, and in every case the thief had entered through a north-facing window. Your safety is worth the price of one or two fewer windows in your home.

You need to protect yourself against trouble, but you shouldn't go overboard. Taoists recommend refraining from buying a gun or other weapon or keeping one in the house. The Taoist opinion is that if you have a gun, then you are expecting someone to come approach you to do you harm. If you don't have a weapon, you are not expecting misfortune to befall. If you have a gun at home, you will meet with robberies. Giving mental energy to a fear can energize it into coming true. Also, more logically, if someone comes up to you and you pull out a gun that you are unable to use with skill, it would probably tip your aggressor's violent tendencies over the edge.

The same thing holds for the martial arts. If you choose to learn them, you would really have to master their disciplines. If you don't master the martial arts and you go out there trying to use them, this could lead you to death or serious injury. Right now, new martial arts schools are opening all the time, but this is America. You have to realize that before the Cultural Revolution, if you opened a martial arts school in China, it meant you were in danger all the time and death could meet you around any corner you turned. Back then, it was normal and legal for anyone who wished to do battle with a person who opened a school for fighting. Opening a school meant sending out a challenge to test your skill. Many people would get hurt. Symbols of the martial arts, such as swords and sabers, should not be hung on the walls of your home, especially higher than your head, no matter how serious you may be about studying the martial arts. Even if you practice for strictly spiritual reasons, you never know what the sight of a sword can touch off in a violent stranger's mind. Keep your martial arts weapons tucked away in a closet when you are not training with them.

Other sources of problems around the house are columns and beamed ceilings. As noted earlier, their sharp edges send out lines of invasive Qi that disrupt the harmony of your home (fig. 137). Low ceilings, beams, and overhangs always affect your health. In an office or place of business, they also harm your finances. Having a flat, plain ceiling without a lot of moldings or decorations is always best. Dr. Wu once recommended that a very elegant new restaurant remove the grid-

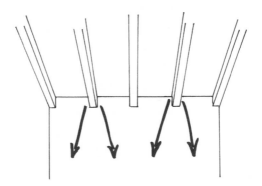

FIGURE. 137

like dropped ceiling that was a centerpiece of the design. He told the owners that if they didn't get rid of it right away, the business would close down within three months. The grid was like a cage. Trapped in a cage, there is no way to prosper. They didn't change the ceiling, and after three and a half months, they were out of business. Sometimes when you read the Feng Shui, you are able to predict how long it will take for something to happen.

If you have a skylight in a ceiling, you need to make sure the ceiling is painted a light, neutral color. Also, don't put carpeting on your ceiling or walls. It's very important to leave things in their natural state. What belongs to the floor should be left on the floor and vice versa. Looking up at a dark ceiling with a skylight opening to bright daylight will create a very jarring effect. You need to go with the flow.

For instance, if you take off your shoes when in the house to keep the floors and carpets clean, you need to take them off outside of the house and keep them there. If you remove your shoes in the entrance hall, you are defeating the purpose of taking them off in the first place. You are still bringing into your house the bad luck that their dirtiness represents. If you don't believe shoes are unclean, then none of this would apply. A large portion of Feng Shui operates on the principle of the great psychological and emotional impact that the resonance of one's surroundings has on one's life. There are some very basic archetypes that live in the minds of people all over the world. These are a few of the natural laws that form the basis of Taoist Feng Shui.

Offices

Most all of the rules of Taoist Feng Shui for the home apply equally to the workplace. Besides the basic difference of incoming Qi versus outgoing Qi, the techniques presented here are the same for private homes and small businesses. Feng Shui for large corporations and for companies that employ over forty-five persons have other rules that are beyond the scope of this book. For helping yourself and your friends and family, the most fundamental principles have been covered. When doing Feng Shui for your office, though, there are a few special factors that must be considered.

To summarize the main points that differ in the office and the home:

1. The position of the front door to your office (or windows above the fifth floor) must allow incoming Qi to enter in the direction of your birth season. If your birth direction is west, Qi must flow in from the east to the west.
2. Faucets are not acceptable in an office. Water running through an office is never considered "incoming."
3. Fish or birds in the office must be in the birth color of the woman of the family.

In addition to these key points, the most important aspect of an office is the position of your desk. Put it in the same position as your birth direction, if possible. Similar Qi goes together; one seeks out the other. Your desk should not face a bathroom. The desk that belongs to the head of the office should not face the front door. Also, your desk should have a solid wall behind it. A glass wall, mirror, or window is not good. You want to be able to feel like you can lean back as far as you want with a sense of security and stability. This means that if you have any trouble, you can step back from it safely. As mentioned in Chapter 6, keeping a crystal ball proportionate in size to your desk in its right-hand corner opposite your seat, aids focus, clarity, and luck. (As a side note, the position of your children's study table at home is also very important. If they are doing poorly in school, check the position of their desk. According to Dr. Wu's *I Ching* calculations, from 1992 to 2003, your child's desk should face southeast. This will be very good for your kids.) If possible, keep the front door of your business wide

open at all times during business hours. This will help customers and clients—as well as the Qi—to find you.

The size of your business's sign should be in direct proportion to your office and building size, never too big or too small. The higher up in a building an office is located, the smaller the sign should be. If the sign is too big, it will give you the feeling that your head is too heavy for your neck to carry. Often, when a store or office has large display windows out front, the tendency is to fill them with signs. This isn't good. Keeping the signs simple and the windows uncluttered will bring in better Qi (fig. 138).

Your Wealth Position

As noted in the discussion of crystals in Chapter 6, one of the most important things you can do to improve the Feng Shui of your home is to stimulate the wealth positions within it. The easiest way to do this is to put coins in all four corners of your house or office. Find as many four-cornered locations as you can. Put money in the four corners inside, in the four corners outside, and in the four corners of every room and it will bring you more fortune. Silver dollars are best, but quarters, nickels, or even pennies will do in a pinch.

The Taoist way of thinking about wealth is summed up in this Chinese folk saying: "Sow melons, harvest melons; sow beans, harvest beans; sow money, harvest money." By putting money down in all the four-cornered locations of your home or office, you let the universe know wealth is your wish. In magical thinking, you want to send out a clear vibration of what you want, to nourish and strengthen that wish daily, and to wait with implicit faith to receive a message back from the universe. In Chinese homes, a picture of the character for luck is hung upside down in a noticeable place. Then, when people come in and asks you why the picture is upside down, they are actually sending you a great blessing. They have just started to think about your luck, and by saying the word, they have emphasized it even more. All this helps to strengthen your own thought vibration. Don't look down on this concept as a superstitious old wives' tale. Modern people have only just begun to recognize the power of directed thought. With the practice of Taoist Feng Shui, you are putting that power into action.

As we have seen, the main wealth position in your house is the first spot your eye comes in contact with when you open your front door at a forty-five degree angle (fig. 139). Putting a light, a crystal ball, or even a statue of the Buddha in this spot can do you much good. In one example, Dr. Wu visited a computer company's warehouse, and upon opening the door at a forty-five degree angle, the first thing he saw was a jumbled pile of wood, right there in the wealth position. He told the owners to clear out that spot immediately. They did, and the very next day they started receiving sizable new orders. For other

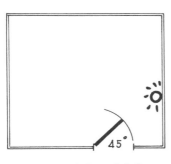

FIGURE. 139

clients, Dr. Wu found that their oldest son's room opened immediately onto a "hostile" angle. Recently, their son had been having problems at work and in his personal life. Dr. Wu suggested that they remove the door and reverse the hinges so the door would open in the opposite direction. This would also open up the space where a table with a crystal ball would need to go.

Finally, to end with a funny story, Dr. Wu once was invited to a popular Chinese nightclub to read its Feng Shui. He noticed a big Buddha statue in the wealth position. Dr. Wu told the owners, "This is a disco. What do you need with a Buddha?" He recommended that they replace the Buddha with a statue of Zhu Bajie, the jolly pig/priest from the Chinese classic novel *Journey to the West*. A rough, lusty sidekick of the Monkey King, Zhu Bajie was beloved by young and old for his capacity to eat, drink, and carouse. Dr. Wu also recommended that the cocktail waiters keep a small Bajie in their apron pockets. They would sell plenty of drinks and their tips would go sky high. The nightclub owners were delighted with all their new business. Making the right Feng Shui connections is all it takes (fig. 140).

FIGURE. 140

9

The Ethics of a
Feng Shui Master

Dr. Wu has found in his nearly forty years of Feng Shui study that the more one learns of it, the more deliberate one becomes when practicing it. The levels of understanding reach down so deeply that one must apply increasing amounts of attention and respect to each new insight. It's like learning to drive a car. The more experienced a driver is, the more careful he or she is on the road. An inexperienced driver is brave and less careful, driving fast and taking risks, not realizing where this impetuousness might lead. The more Feng Shui readings

Dr. Wu does, the more cautious he becomes. He knows that even a small mistake can lead a client in the wrong direction. Not only is he bound to a sense of responsibility toward his clients; he also carries that over to what he is willing to teach. He insists on a standard of absolute safety and effectiveness of the material he presents, realizing that even with all of his experience with the I Ching and Feng Shui, there is still so much to learn. The study of the laws of heaven and earth is a lifetime undertaking.

After years of study in the White Cloud Monastery under Master Du Xinlin, Dr. Wu was chosen by the great Feng Shui Master Qian Dong Shu to be his personal student. Master Qian, a respected authority who was known throughout China as the first leader in the field of Feng Shui, would never come out and call himself a master. He would never boast of his expertise, even though he had studied Feng Shui his entire life. Similarly, Dr. Wu feels that he would rather present a paper at a medical conference attended by hundreds of people than casually teach a small Feng Shui class. When you practice Feng Shui, what you are doing is revealing the information you have received from heaven. The responsibility of this knowledge requires great care. The more you study, and the more you tell others, the more you begin to question yourself. "Is it right?" "Am I presenting this information correctly and clearly?" The practice of Feng Shui requires a level of commitment and soul searching that only the most sincere souls can accept.

Even just the discipline involved in the daily practice of Qi Gong is a difficult test. It is the first requirement of a true Feng Shui practitioner. Without building sensitivity to the Qi in your body, a proper awareness of the powerful forces of the universe cannot be achieved. The entire system of Chinese astrology, numerology, and I Ching divination, as well as all the compasses and mathematical calculations, were derived from the teachings of the towering spiritual masters of antiquity. Nevertheless, the complexities and intellectual rigors of this system belie the simple truths one directly attunes with in daily Qi Gong practice.

Even more important than sensitizing the body, the proper practice of Qi Gong must be focused on training one's heart. In the White Cloud Monastery, when one wanted to leave to practice Feng Shui in the outside world, regardless of how many years one had been spent there, a holy vow had to be taken. To swear to this oath means taking on the heart of the Buddha:

> Your mind and heart must unite as one, in harmony with the universe and all living creatures. You renounce selfishness, for in each thought of personal interest, good and bad intentions coexist. You swear to maintain a big heart, a merciful heart and a kind heart, even to the insects that crawl at your feet. Anyone who hears the word of enlightenment must dedicate themselves to the cultivation of kindness and good. Anyone who listens to the word will gain wisdom. If you know the Buddha's heart, you have already attained the Tao.

The oath is easy to say but very difficult to accomplish. When you do Qi Gong and Feng Shui, you act as an agent of God. You must accept this vow upon yourself. You must possess the ability to sacrifice yourself for all. You must have the courage to go down to hell, so that you may come back and help. In order to perform Feng Shui for others, these thoughts must be foremost in your mind. You have to possess the ability to transform evil into good inside of yourself first, before you can transform it in the world around you.

Dr. Wu's grandfather, a highly respected doctor and imperial physician, had two students who rose to become great doctors of their generation. One, Kong Bohua, was very scholarly and intellectual. Dr. Wu's grandfather would have him study the old volumes of medical texts, and augmented his studies with personal training. The other student, Xiao Longyou, nicknamed "Little Maybe, Maybe Not," was the door attendant at the house. Whenever Dr. Wu's grandfather would make the rounds of his patients, Little Maybe, Maybe Not would follow along. He was just a humble servant with little education. Whenever he accompanied his teacher, the respected doctor would make him shovel the horse manure out of the street, bury the dead animals frozen at the roadsides in the cold Beijing winters, and help dress and arrange the dead patients in their shrouds. This menial labor went on for ten years, when finally Little Maybe, Maybe Not asked the doctor why he had never taught him anything in all that time. Doctor Wu's grandfather answered him by saying, "Don't talk like that. All these years I had you do good deeds; ten whole years of them. You will find out how much you have learned."

There are two types of doctors. "Book doctors" build their practice on the techniques and intellectual knowledge they use to treat patients. The other kind is called an "ethical doctor." These doctors may never have had any formal education. They may not even know how to read or write, and yet they heal their patients successfully, time and again. Little Maybe, Maybe Not was taught to be an ethical doctor. In the end, he became even more famous than Kong Bohua, the scholarly student. The two of them stayed in Dr. Wu's grandfather's house for fifteen years. They were both told they could go out and practice at the same time. They had both been taught all that the elder Dr. Wu had to give.

Eventually, Little Maybe, Maybe Not's fame as a doctor surpassed that of Dr. Kong. Dr. Xiao would just touch his patients and they would get well. People who couldn't find a successful treatment anywhere else would come to Dr. Xiao. He would lay his hands on them and they would be cured. If Dr. Wu hadn't seen it with his own eyes, he would hardly have been able to believe it, either.

Today most medical training emphasizes accepted knowledge and techniques. There's not enough emphasis on the ethical underpinnings of the healing arts. Sometimes, it's more important to be a good person than just to have knowledge and techniques. This is not to say that you shouldn't try to read broadly and learn as much as you can.

Don't disregard the books and practical methodology. Besides this knowledge, though, there exists another level of ability on which heartfelt intention and prayer work. As a boy, Dr. Wu knew Dr. Xiao and he can tell you that he couldn't read or write even a few words. If you asked him where a particular acupuncture point was he wouldn't be able to tell you. Still he became a very famous doctor, much more well known than his teacher, Dr. Wu's grandfather. Of the four most celebrated doctors of China, Dr. Xiao is considered the top one.

Whether you are a doctor or a martial artist or a student of Qi Gong and Feng Shui, you must always have a good heart and good ethics. Some doctors have excellent cure rates, while their academic careers are not that bright. They are most likely ethical doctors. Sometimes, graduating from a top school and earning an M.D. or a Ph.D., or both, will not help you treat patients out in the real world. There are blind doctors who cannot see their patients and yet are able to effect a cure. Having a kind, ethical heart is more important than having all the book learning in the world.

To be a Feng Shui master means accepting a grave responsibility. Your primary goal is living in unity with the forces of nature. In a sense, you must renounce the social and cultural shells that most people live securely within, in order to emerge as a force of nature yourself. Esoteric Taoist philosophy advocates this as the supreme achievement of the spiritually adept. A person cannot hope to manipulate the basic building blocks of the universe, the forces of Yin and Yang, without becoming one with the cosmos. Take, for example, the Jin Gan Bu Huai practice discussed in Chapter 5. The techniques may not be that difficult to explain, but mastering the actual meditative experience is very challenging. You have to reach down into the depths of your soul to find the strength of mind and the fullness of heart to accomplish the purification. If your ethical nature is not spotless and the light from your body is not shining and your heart is not filled with the most exalted sentiments, how do you expect to change the Qi? Taoist Feng Shui, at its roots, is about taking the Qi of nature into your body. Using the power of consciousness, your body becomes the crucible in which the positive forces of the heavens are called down to cleanse the unrefined energy of the earth. This is cosmic alchemy on the grandest scale.

A Feng Shui practitioner must be able to accomplish all of this while also retaining a sense of simple humility. The masters of ancient China, before they would arrange their alter to begin the rites of battle and sacrifice, would recite a private oath: "Dan Mo Ming Xing Zhi," or "Bland surface replacing brilliant appearance." It means you are far away from fame. You are not looking for prestige. If you are seeking fame, fortune, and profit, you cannot become a Feng Shui master. A famous fortune-teller in the local Chinese community told Dr. Wu he was forming a Taoist association and appointing himself its president. Dr. Wu asked him, "If you are the president, who's going to be the Feng Shui master?" One of the vows of the Feng Shui initiate is to renounce all political offices and titles. If you held an official political position, you would have to concern yourself with thoughts of authority and political advantage. This sort of power-oriented thinking creates Ba Qi (stopped Qi) in the body, which clouds the Original Energy and thereby disrupts the ability to harmonize with nature. Birds are so sensitive to Ba Qi that they can feel it from more than three feet away and will fly from you.

As a Feng Shui practitioner, you can also run a business or be a doctor or lawyer or do any type of work you please, as long as it's not involved with politics. Humbleness is a very important quality that needs to be constantly reinforced. Don't run after glory, always coveting things that aren't yours to have. You need to be quiet and calm (dan) in order to read Feng Shui properly. Dr. Wu has seen flashy advertisements on television for Feng Shui practitioners that use the "subtlety" of a used car salesperson, urging people to come on down to the office and watch the miracles fly. This type of advertising is completely against the heavenly laws of Feng Shui. Moderate advertising, just enough to get the word out, is all right. The people who need you will find you. Don't overdo it. Feng Shui practitioners must be modest about their accomplishments and low-key about calling attention to themselves. If you break these laws, such as by manipulating, cheating, or taking advantage of others, financially or otherwise, it will come back to you.

This is not to say that you cannot charge a fee for your Feng Shui readings. People who employ Feng Shui practitioners are seeking to change their fate. To gain something, you must give something. This is a basic Taoist philosophy. Charge what you feel your skill level deserves. The concept of giving something back also holds true for the Feng Shui practitioner. Three days before a reading, they must remove all meat from their diet. On the day of the reading, the practitioner must cleanse his body and fast the entire day. These are heavenly rules. They must not be broken. The day Dr. Wu goes out to do a Feng Shui reading or any other serious undertaking, he takes great care to fast. Afterward, he buys bread and goes to the ocean to feed the birds. He has to compensate for any damage he may have done. When you help something, you also break something. You must make up for what you have broken.

You cannot keep all of the money you earn for doing a reading. You must take a meaningful amount and give it away. If you do not release some of this money, you will never achieve complete success. Whatever comes in to you, you must allow some of it to go out. No matter what price you ask for, you must give some of it back. Dr. Wu does this by taking the percentage he has chosen and leaving it in small bills lying on the sidewalk. Thus, he is helping others in a humble way, without seeking admiration for his charity. This law of give-and-take is even symbolized in the Feng Shui of a house. If you are making money, you need to make sure your house has a back door or window. Otherwise, the money has nowhere to flow out, and on a subconscious level, can make you sick. It is very important that the rule of giving come from the heart.

As noted in Chapter 3, one of the great ancient masters of Feng Shui, Zhu Ge Liang, was the military advisor and general. If "Dan Mo

Ming Xing Zi" was his oath, how did he allow himself to be the general and chief advisor to the emperor and to help the government with military endeavors, all of which is contrary to the principle of Feng Shui? At first, he had not wanted to be involved. He rebuffed the emperor's command three times before he agreed to help. Because he bowed to the command of the emperor to help the nation, rather than uphold the vows of a Taoist adept, his life was cut short. His original fate decreed that he would live to the age of seventy-six. Because he broke his vow, his life was shortened by twenty-two years. When helping someone, you must have the wisdom to give them only the information they need. You don't want to overwhelm them. Also, it is unwise to overexpose them to this information because it comes from the secrets of heaven, which are supposed to remain hidden. If you reveal too much of this secret wisdom, you will cut short your own life. Do things moderately and keep things to the point. Though fate and destiny can be modified, even the wisest master cannot hope to alter the main pathway of its flow. Challenging this truth is no different than challenging one's own soul.

To be a Feng Shui master is to help humanity and work for spiritual growth. It is a challenging and serious responsibility, but it is also an opportunity to contribute to society. The seven stories of the Pagoda symbolize the levels of spiritual accomplishment available to humans (fig. 141). On the first level is to do good things for people as a regular person might—not harming anyone, but not necessarily going out of the way to make a big difference, either. The next level is to bury dead cats that are found lying at the side of the road to set their souls free, and on the third level the same is done for dead dogs. On the fourth level is to be a matchmaker, introducing people to each other who become happy couples. Also on the fourth level is the practice of Qi Gong. The fifth level of service is to bury

FIGURE. 141

a bird, and the sixth level involves making contributions to culture or society as a doctor, a scientist, an inventor, or a virtuoso musician, for instance.

The seventh and highest level of spiritual accomplishment is to save a person's life, rescuing someone from drowning or from a burning house. If you have ever been in a life-threatening situation such as this, you have been given a blessed opportunity for advancement. The Feng Shui practitioner is a doctor of the earth. If you simply study Feng Shui by doing Qi Gong, without applying your knowledge to actual conditions, you are still participating in an act that is on the fourth level of achievement. If you are a practicing Feng Shui master, you have already reached the sixth level. It is an honor bestowed from heaven to have this ability.

Just as there are Five Elements—fire, water, wood, metal, and earth—there are five moral disciplines that the student of Feng Shui must live by. These are the Five Virtues of Confucius: XIN, REN, YI, LI, and ZHI, which refer to ethics, natural talent, training, trustworthiness, and propriety, respectively. The number-one requirement for a Feng Shui master is to have an ethical heart. This is XIN, which corresponds to fire. We have discussed this principle at length. Be kind, fair, and honest. Don't cheat people or practice Feng Shui just to make money. Charge only what you feel your skills are worth. Pray for others and wish them well, and always give something back.

REN is one's natural ability to perform Feng Shui. This virtue corresponds to earth. Not everybody can be a doctor or psychiatrist or a Feng Shui master. You have to have a special gift. YI is training, it corresponds to wood. You need to have special training to bring out your natural gifts, just as a tree grows from the earth. After you have been properly trained, you can go out to help others.

LI is trustworthiness. You can't just move from one place to another, and then three months later, move again. If people have questions or need help, they have to know how to find you. Be stable. If you can't treat a client's house, you need to tell the client straight out. Don't give the client a story, like he or she came to you too late to be helped. If you can't do it, you can't do it. You must be honest. This virtue corresponds to the element of metal.

The fifth virtue, ZHI, corresponding to water, is propriety. You must have manners. Respect your teachers and your elders. Take care of your parents. Dr. Wu has patients in their eighties and nineties who are completely alone. Their children never visit or have anything to do with them. The Chinese perspective is that you can move out of a tight family circle but you can never stop helping your parents. Some people say, "My parents have money; they might as well hire someone to take care of them. They're not going to leave me an inheritance, so why should I help them?" This is not the Chinese way. No matter what, you must always help your parents, whether or not they have been good to you. Aiding your family is the human way. Practicing good manners will lead you to greater wisdom.

Another aspect of ZHI is to present yourself well. The last time Dr. Wu visited Hong Kong, he met with the four top Feng Shui masters in the city and noticed that there seemed to be some sort of fashion statement going on. They were all dressed like the ancient Chinese, masters, having long hair and beards and wearing robes that at best could be called "unique." He wondered whether their reputations were just hype. An outlandish appearance goes against the Feng Shui master's injunctions to be humble and modest. It's not as if you can get into your car, drive to a client's house, and then quickly throw on a magic robe and a Taoist hat. This is not what makes your readings accurate. The Feng Shui needs to come from within.

This leads us to reiterate that the material presented in this book is basic information designed to introduce the reader to the remarkable world of Taoist Feng Shui. The techniques discussed here, though basic, should be used to help yourself, your family, and your friends. They are not meant to be used professionally. If you are in good health, with all of your senses, limbs, and organs intact, you may never become a master of Feng Shui. The special sensitivities that are necessary for proper understanding and accuracy are found in only two classes of people—people with physical handicaps and people who have been chosen by a decree of heaven. Dr. Wu has presented this material so you can improve your own life. It is worthwhile to study Feng Shui and practice Qi Gong, no matter what else you do for a living. You even might find you have a natural calling, and then it would be appropriate to find someone who is a true Feng Shui and Qi Gong master who can help supervise your growth.

People who are physically challenged make up the first category of accurate Feng Shui practitioners. The practice of Qi Gong and Feng Shui helps them with their disabilities and with the obstacles they face in our society. It is also a way for them to earn a living while also putting their special talents to use. The reason people with disabilities are so accurate at reading Feng Shui is found in the Taoist laws of balance. For example, if someone is blind, the heart will be strengthened. A strong heart allows one to read the inner secrets of the Tao. Similarly, if someone has a problem with his or her legs, the hands become more sensitive. This is the balance of Yin and Yang. To adjust for the physical limitations, heaven declares that intuition, sensitivity, and psychic ability become stronger. Hence, the ability to predict becomes stronger as well.

The other type of person who may practice Feng Shui professionally is one who has been designated by heaven. This person must commit his or her entire life to the cultivation of Qi Gong. You either you have this gift or you don't. You must study the *I Ching* and practice Qi Gong to know whether you have this gift. If you do, you will have many wonderful opportunities to help people wherever you may go. If you don't, at least you will know. Then, you can spend your time following pursuits that will be a fuller expression of your own unique capabilities. Each of us has a contribution to make in this world. Discover your true nature by practicing Qi Gong.

Through the practice of Qi Gong, we become helpers of God. We promote peace on earth by cultivating it within ourselves. As we merge with the breath of the universe, the planet is healed by our shared union. Riding the waves of Qi, our consciousness is opened to the vastness of time and space and to the truths of universal law. Perhaps the most profound revelations on this journey into Taoist Feng Shui is the realization of our own innate potential for creative thought.

What is illumination, really? The most basic universal truth, the true light of the mind, is found no more or less than in the limitless possibilities of your imagination. It is the bridge between you and your world, and whatever lies beyond. Your creativity is the foundation of your heart and mind, the birth right of every person on earth. May it flow like the winds of heaven and the waters of the ocean, stand firm like the mountain, and soar like the bird. And may the spark that shines within burn like the fiery Eyes of the Dragon.

Index

Mystic Practice (Mi Lien), 66–7
practice the Heart Secret with
the, 63–6
Mountain(s)
forest of the, 54–5
trigram, 28, 30, 33
Mouth Secret, 72–6
Mudras, 76–7
Mystic Practice, 66–7, 104

National Bank of China Building,
13, 35
Nature, communicating with the
forces of and following the
patterns of, 8, 15–18, 31, 54,
66, 104, 107–41, 197
Neighborhood, choosing an ideal
location for your home or
office, 151–7
Nien Li, 104
Nine, the number, 29, 31
Nine Palaces, 8
Numbers/numerology, role of, 19–40
fortunate, 28–9, 32
testing the wind, 36–8
3-6-72 formula, 32–6
Numbers that make up your birth
date act as a powerful talisman, 22–3

Office
adjusting the inside of, to
stimulate health and wealth,
167, 169–70
bad layouts, 163–5
bathrooms, 177
business sign, 189
choosing employees, 150
choosing size, 149–50
clear crystal ball in, 140, 177, 188
doing Feng Shui for, 187–91
hallways and storage space, 177–9
horses and, 116
importance of neighborhood, 151–7
incoming and outgoing Qi, 179–82
miscellaneous building elements
to consider, 182–7
numbers and, 30
3-6-72 formula for finding, 32–6
using children to check an, 45–6
where to position, 32–9, 145–7
One, the number, 28, 29, 31

Orange trees, 129
Original Qi, 56, 57, 71
Orthodox School of Taoist Feng
Shui (Mi Zong Feng Shui), 2, 4
Ox, 37, 96

Pei, I. M., 13
Peng Tzi, 103
Personal birth direction, 21–3
Pig, 37, 96
Plant life
sharing with plants, 122–30
talking to plants, etc., 66, 104
see also Mind Secret
Prayer ritual, 104–5
Principle of correspondences, 110
Pyramid, influence of the, 163–4

Qi, 5, 7–10, 16, 17, 19, 29, 30,
145, 147, 148–51, 158, 167–9,
177–9, 182
absorbing plant, 123–4
blocked, 57, 75, 153, 198
building your, practicing the
Five Mystic Codes, 62–75
elements of the Five Forests emit,
50–7
incoming and outgoing, 179–82,
187–9
mineral elements and, 135–7
offices and, 188–91
principle of correspondences, 110
sensing the, 41–57, 140–1
to test the, 36–9, 151
training your body's, 83–6
Qian Dong Shu, 194
Qian Kun Gua (the Heaven and Earth
hexagram), 32
Qian trigram, 103
Qi Gong physical training techniques
and healing, 2–3, 8–10, 15–18,
36, 37, 53, 68, 75, 109, 149,
153, 174, 194–5, 197, 200–4
cultivation and practice, 87–8
exorcism, 94–105
Five Centers, 8
Five Forests, 50–7
Five Mystic Codes, 62–75
hand seals, 76–9
lunar, 8, 10
mineral kingdom and, 130–41